I0410339

United States
Department of
Agriculture

Forest Service

Pacific Northwest
Research Station

Resource Bulletin
PNW-RB-253
May 2007

Forest Resources of the Umatilla National Forest

Glenn A. Christensen, Paul Dunham, David C. Powell, and Bruce Hiserote

Authors

Glenn A. Christensen is an inventory analyst, and **Bruce Hiserote** is a forester, Pacific Northwest Research Station, 620 SW Main Street, Suite 400, Portland, OR 97205; **Paul Dunham** is a forest health analyst, Forest Health Protection, Pacific Northwest Region, P.O. Box 3623, Portland, OR 97208; **David C. Powell** is a silviculturist, Umatilla National Forest, 2517 SW Hailey Avenue, Pendleton, OR 97801.

Cover: Umatilla National Forest, photograph by Paul Dunham.

Abstract

**Christensen, Glenn A.; Dunham, Paul; Powell, David C.; Hiserote, Bruce.
2007.** Forest resources of the Umatilla National Forest. Resour. Bull. PNW-
RB-253. Portland, OR: U.S. Department of Agriculture, Forest Service, Pacific
Northwest Research Station. 38 p.

Current resource statistics for the Umatilla National Forest, based on two separate
inventories conducted in 1993–96 and in 1997–2002, are presented in this report.
Currently on the Umatilla National Forest, 89 percent of the land area is classified
as forest land. The predominant forest type is grand fir (26 percent of forested
acres) followed by the interior Douglas-fir (25 percent) and ponderosa pine (17
percent) types. The majority of net cubic foot wood volume (55 percent) comes from
trees ranging in size from 11 to 23 inches diameter at breast height. The most commonly recorded cause of tree death was bark beetle (primarily *Dendroctonus* spp.)
attack, with over half of the mortality volume attributed to these insects.

Keywords: Umatilla National Forest, forest inventory, Blue Mountains, Current
Vegetation Survey.

Summary

Updated resource statistics for the Umatilla National Forest are presented in this report. The last forest resource inventory information compiled for the Umatilla National Forest was completed in the early 1980s. Two relatively recent inventories (1993–96 and 1997–2002) using a grid-based sampling system prompted this analysis and report describing the current vegetation of the Umatilla National Forest. This report provides a broad overview of land status, forest structure and composition, and forest health and productivity. Key findings are:

- Currently on the Umatilla National Forest, 89 percent of the land area is classified as forest land.

- The predominant forest type is grand fir (26 percent of forested acres) followed by the interior Douglas-fir (25 percent) and ponderosa pine (17 percent) types.

- The most common tree species on the forest is grand fir (*Abies grandis* (Dougl. ex D. Don) Lindl.); 32 percent of all trees (1.0 inch diameter at breast height [d.b.h.] and larger) are grand fir trees. The next most numerous tree species are lodgepole pine (*Pinus contorta* Dougl. ex Loud.) and Douglas-fir (*Pseudotsuga menziesii* (Mirbel) Franco) at 24 percent and 15 percent, respectively, of all trees greater than 1.0 inch d.b.h.

- The majority of net cubic foot wood volume (55 percent) comes from trees ranging in size from 11 to 23 inches d.b.h.

- The current total net volume of wood in live trees on the forest is estimated to be in excess of 14.0 billion board feet (± 6 percent standard error).

- By species, grand fir, Douglas-fir, and ponderosa pine (*Pinus ponderosa* P. & C. Lawson) contribute 76 percent of the total board foot volume. The two next most important species are western larch (*Larix occidentalis* Nutt.) and Engelmann spruce (*Picea engelmannii* Parry ex Engelm.), contributing 11 percent and 10 percent, respectively, of the total volume.

- Overall, forest-land acreage averages 2.7 snags per acre greater than 20 inches d.b.h. Within the grand fir forest type, snags this size average 5 per acre with only 1 per acre in the "recent" decay class.

- On average, there are 3.7 down logs per acre greater than 20 inches diameter on forest land. Within the grand fir forest type, there are about 5 down logs per acre this size.

- The most commonly recorded cause of tree death was bark beetle (primarily *Dendroctonus* spp.) attack, with over half of the mortality volume attributed to these insects.
- Wildfire risk assessment indicates that within the subalpine fir (*Abies lasiocarpa* (Hook.) Nutt.) and Engelmann spruce forest types more than half of the acres (64 percent for subalpine fir and 61 percent for Engelmann spruce) have a torching index that is less than 20 miles per hour of windspeed, indicating that a large proportion of these types are at high risk of wildfire torching.

Contents

Introduction

Current forest resource statistics for the Umatilla National Forest (UNF) are presented in this report. The last forest resource inventory information compiled for the forest was completed in 1981 (Teply 1981). In the early 1990s, a grid-based sampling strategy was adopted for broad-scale inventory and monitoring of forest and range vegetation on National Forest System lands in the Pacific Northwest Region (Max et al. 1996).

Two relatively recent inventories (1993–96 and 1997–2002) using the new grid-based system prompted this analysis and report describing the current vegetation of the UNF. This report provides a broad overview of land status, forest structure and composition, and forest health and productivity as follows:

- Land status
- Forest structure and composition
    - Acres of forest by forest type
    - Numbers of trees by species and size
    - Basal area by forest type
    - Forest-land area by stand-size class

- Forest health and productivity
    - Biomass of live, standing dead, and down logs by forest type and stand size
    - Volume of wood by tree species
    - Number of snags and down logs by forest type and tree species
    - Insect and disease incidence by tree species and forest type
    - Wildfire risk assessment
    - Forest growth and mortality by tree species
    - Site class by forest type

The Umatilla National Forest, located in the northern portion of the Blue Mountains in northeastern Oregon and southeastern Washington, includes 1,406,513 acres of National Forest System land (fig. 1). Over 20 percent of these lands occur in designated wilderness areas. The headwaters of three large drainage basins are within the forest: the Middle Columbia, the Lower Snake, and the John Day. The forest also has many rivers and streams including portions of the Grande Ronde, Umatilla, and North Fork John Day Rivers.

Topography of the northern Blue Mountains features thick basalt bedrock deposited during molten basalt flows originating from long fissure vents in the northeastern Blue Mountains (Clarke and Bryce 1997). This Columbia River basalt

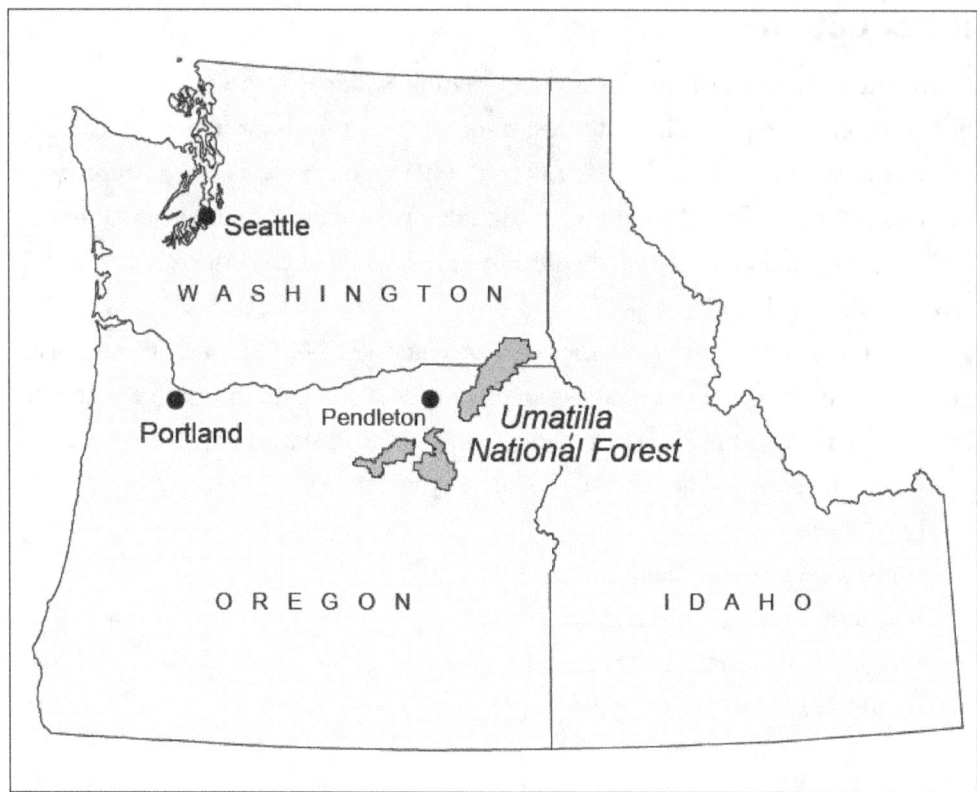

Figure 1–Location of the Umatilla National Forest.

has weathered to create rugged mountains, steep canyons, and extensive ridges and plateaus (fig. 2) (Anderson et al. 1998).

Elevations within the UNF range from 1,700 to 7,900 ft. Natural disturbance processes on the forest include wildfire, insects, and disease. Owing to recent wildfires and insect outbreaks (table 1), the Blue Mountains have become a focal point of forest health issues (Johnson 1994, Mutch et al. 1993, Quigley 1992, Tanaka et al. 1995, Wickman 1992).

Methods and Inventory Procedures

The two most recent inventories on the UNF were conducted by using an inventory and monitoring system called the Current Vegetation Survey (CVS) (Johnson 1998, 2001; Max et al. 1996). Land managers use CVS data to assess and monitor vegetation at known locations. The CVS plots are arranged on a regularly spaced grid at 1.7-mi intervals across nonwilderness lands and 3.4 mi across wilderness lands. Each CVS plot contains five 0.05-acre subplots, with one subplot located at plot center, and the remaining four subplots 133.9 ft from center on cardinal directions. At the time of the first plot installation, the plot design was a 185.1-ft-radius circle

Figure 2—Open stand of ponderosa pine on a steep canyon slope formed from weathered Columbia River basalt, Umatilla National Forest.

Table 1—Recent disturbance events on the Umatilla National Forest by causal agent

Year	Defoliators (budworm, tussock moth)	Bark beetles (Douglas-fir beetle, fir engraver)	Pine beetles (mountain, western)	Other insects	Wildfires (≥100 acres)
			Thousand acres		
1970–1979	524	403	1,670	8	3
1980–1989	4,180	271	76	2	27
1990–1999	1,794	406	18	12	82
2000–2005	80	171	23	87	40

A note of caution when summing acreages: any individual acre is not exclusive to disturbance by only one causal agent, which means that areas affected by one agent may overlap with areas affected by other agents. An area can also be affected by the same agent in more than one year; for events such as budworm defoliation that often span a multiyear period, this means that the same acreage might be accounted for more than once in the decadal values shown in this table.

Species names: Budworm (*Choristoneura occidentalis* Freeman); tussock moth (*Orgyia pseudotsugata* McDunnough); Douglas-fir beetle (*Dendroctonus pseudotsugae* Hopkins); fir engraver (*Scolytus ventralis* LeConte); mountain pine beetle (*Dendroctonus ponderosae* Hopkins); western pine beetle (*Dendroctonus brevicomis* LeConte).

Source: For defoliators, bark beetles, pine beetles, and other insects, the source was aerial detection survey data; for wildfires, the source was digital fire atlas records, U.S. Department of Agriculture, Forest Service, Umatilla National Forest. 2005. http://www.fs.fed.us/r6/data-library/gis/umatilla/ (January 2007).

containing the cluster of five subplots. Each of the five subplots consisted of nested circles of 51.1-ft, 26.3-ft, and 11.8-ft radii. At the time of remeasurement, the 26.3-ft plot was replaced with a 24-ft-radius plot.

The first inventory (first occasion) was conducted over several field seasons beginning in 1993 and ending in 1996. A total of 640 plots were installed. The second occasion was a remeasurement of first-occasion plots and conducted over a series of four panels, each panel consisting of about 25 percent of the plots. Remeasurement started with panel C in 1997, followed by panel D in 1999, and panel A in 2002 including all wilderness plots. Panel B plot remeasurements were completed in 2005, but the data have not yet been processed. The 490 remeasured plots in panels A, C, and D have been compiled for use as the second-occasion measurement for this report. Except where noted, broad forest overview estimates are based on this second-occasion information. Forest health estimates of growth, mortality, and causes of tree death given in the last part of the report are based on, except where noted, changes occurring between first- and second-occasion measurements of panels A and D. Panel C was not included in this comparison owing to an inability to determine if some trees were not remeasured because of a change in the subplot radius, or because they had fallen. In addition, the time between measurements for much of panel C was often less than 2 years. Estimates of dead wood are based on first-occasion measurements of all four panels; second-occasion estimates of down dead wood had not been completed at the time of this report. All plot data were compiled by using the Pacific Northwest Research Station—Forest Inventory and Analysis Program's integrated database (IDB) format (Waddell and Hiserote 2005).

Reliability of Inventory Data

The sample used for this inventory was designed to meet national standards for precision in state and regional estimates of forest attributes. Standard errors, which denote the precision of an estimate, are usually higher for smaller subsets of the data. Forest-level estimates and standard errors along with standard error by forest type and species for various attributes are provided in each table. Standard errors for other estimates are available upon request. Results are based on the sums of plot data and represent conditions at the broader scale (UNF), and not any specific area or site except for the plot itself.

Land Status

The UNF can be broadly described by land cover and productivity. Land status is classified into the following categories, which are used throughout this report:

- Forest land—Land at least 10 percent stocked with live trees, or land that had this minimum tree stocking in the past and is not currently developed for non-forest use. The minimum area recognized is 1 acre.

- Timberland—Forested area capable of growing continuous stands of trees at a rate of 20 ft^3/acre per year (at culmination of mean annual increment) and not reserved from harvest by law or statute such as in wilderness areas. This is a specific FIA subclassification for areas that are considered "productive forest land." Throughout this report, all forest land is used when presenting summary data, not just forest land considered "productive."

- Wilderness—Land protected from development or commodity production by the 1964 Wilderness Act.

- Nonforest—Land that has never supported forests or formerly was forested and currently is developed for nonforest uses. Included is land used for agriculture crops, Christmas tree farms, cottonwood plantations, improved pasture, residential areas, city parks, constructed roads, operating railroads and their right-of-way clearings, powerline and pipeline clearings, streams more than 30 ft wide, and 1- to 40-acre areas of water classified by the Bureau of the Census, U.S. Department of Commerce, as land. If intermingled in forest areas, unimproved roads and other nonforest strips must be more than 120 ft wide, and clearings or other areas must be 1 acre or larger to qualify as nonforest.

- Other forest land—Forest land that is not reserved or productive enough to be considered timberland.

- Other reserved—Forest land that is not productive enough to be considered timberland and not reserved from timber harvest by law or statute. This includes protected lands such as special interest areas, special botanical areas, wild and scenic river corridors, and wilderness study areas.

Currently, 89 percent of the Umatilla National Forest is classified as forest land.

Currently, 89 percent of the UNF is classified as forest land (1.25 million acres), with 61 percent of the UNF classified as timberland (857,057 acres). On the UNF, there are three wilderness areas comprising 22 percent of the UNF acreage (281,684 acres of forest land and 23,232 acres of nonforest). A total of 119,995 acres is defined as nonforest (9 percent of the total), and 77,825 acres (6 percent of the total) as other forest land (fig. 3). Throughout this report, the forest resource information pertains to all forest land (except where noted), including designated wilderness areas, and excluding areas classified as nonforest.

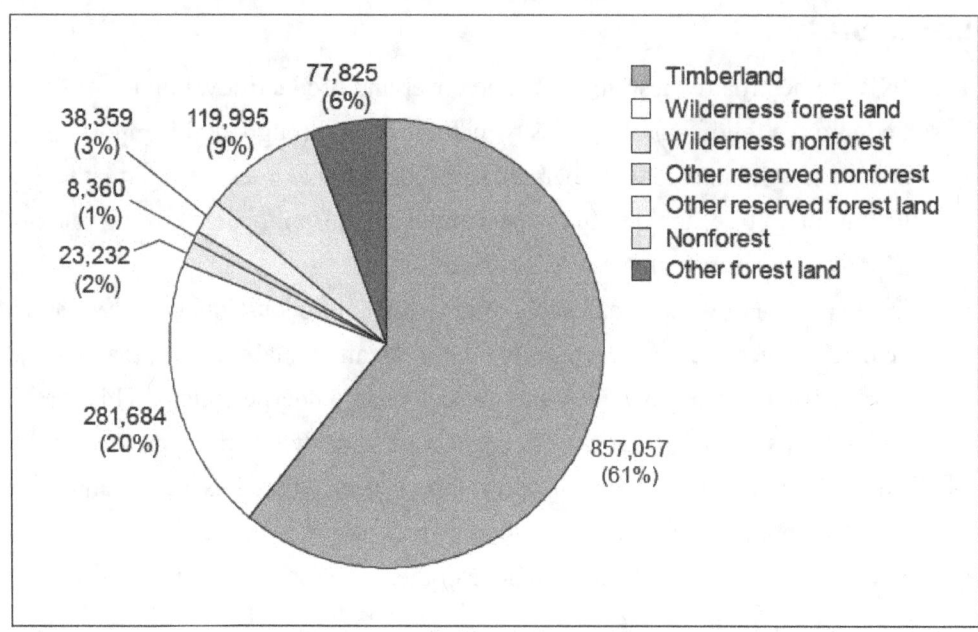

Figure 3—Acres and percentage by land class, Umatilla National Forest, 2002 (occasion 2 data only).

Forest Structure and Composition

Forest Type

Vegetation cover type is described here by using a forest type classification. Forest type is assigned by evaluating the relative proportions of live trees on the plot. The predominant tree species is based on plurality of tree stocking, and the plot area is classified as that forest type.[1] Stocking is an expression of the extent to which growing space is effectively utilized by live trees. If total stocking is determined to be <10 percent, the area is assigned a nonstocked forest type. Table 2 shows how the forest is currently classified by forest type in acres.

On the Umatilla, grand fir and Douglas-fir are the most common forest types (fig. 4) by percentage of total forest-land area. Together these two types occupy slightly more than half of the total forest-land area with grand fir at 26 percent and Douglas-fir at 25 percent (fig. 5).[2] Ponderosa pine is the next most common forest

---

[1] Arner, S.L.; Woudenberg, S.; Waters, S.; Vissage, J.; MacLean, C.; Thompson, M.; Hansen, M. [N.d.]. National algorithms for determining stocking class, stand size class, and forest type for Forest Inventory and Analysis plots. Manuscript in preparation. On file with: G. Christensen, Pacific Northwest Research Station, 620 SW Main St., Suite 400, Portland, OR 97205.

[2] Douglas-fir growing on the Umatilla National Forest and as reported here is interior Douglas-fir (*Pseudotsuga menziesii* var. *glauca* (Beissn.) Franco), not the coastal variety (*Pseudotsuga menziesii* var. *menziesii*) typically found growing west of the Cascade Mountain divide.

Table 2—Forest-land acres by forest type, Umatilla National Forest, 2002 (occasion 2 data only)

Forest type	Total	Standard error	Number of plots with forest type present
	Thousand acres (percent)		
Grand fir	329	28 (8)	131
Douglas-fir	308	26 (8)	142
Ponderosa pine	213	23 (11)	109
Lodgepole pine	77	15 (19)	39
Western larch	75	16 (21)	29
Engelmann spruce	60	13 (22)	27
Subalpine fir	25	8 (32)	11
Western juniper	7	3 (43)	6
Nonstocked	160	18 (11)	100
All types	1,254	17 (1)	

Umatilla National Forest

Figure 4—Grand fir forest type. Grand fir and Douglas-fir are the most common forest types on the Umatilla National Forest.

type with 17 percent of the forest-land area. Other less common forest types include lodgepole pine (6 percent), western larch (6 percent), Engelmann spruce (5 percent), subalpine fir (2 percent), and finally western juniper at less than 1 percent (fig. 6).

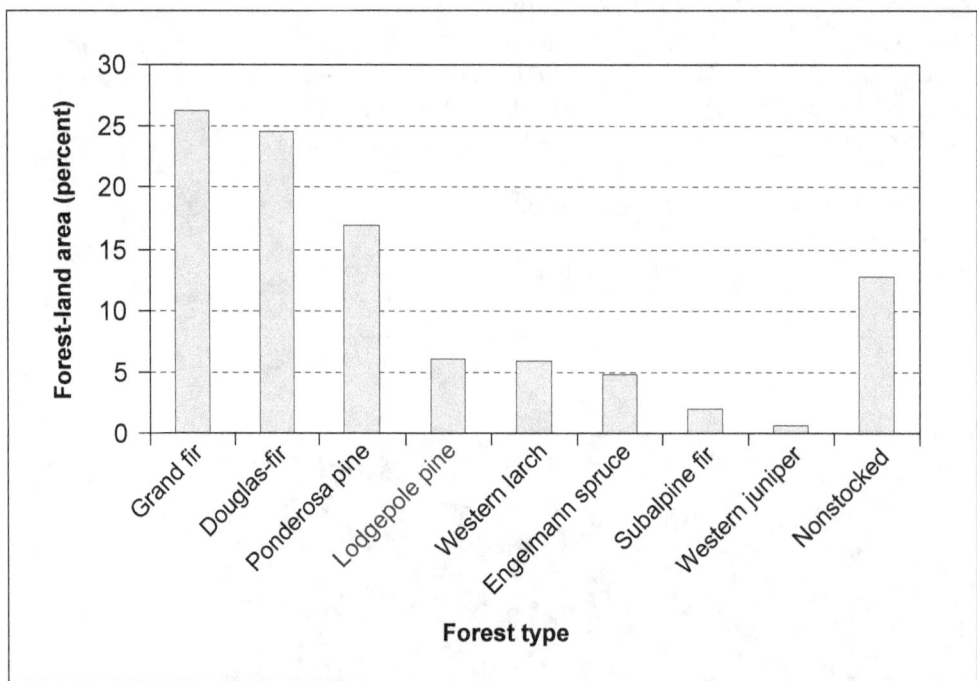

Figure 5—Percentage of forest-land area by forest type, Umatilla National Forest, 2002 (occasion 2 data only).

Figure 6—Western juniper (foreground) is a minor forest type on the Umatilla National Forest.

Species and Size

One method to evaluate current forest composition is to look at the total number of trees by species. Figure 7 shows the estimated number of trees by species classified into three size classes: saplings (ranging in diameter at breast height (d.b.h.) from 1.0 to 5.0 inches), larger pole-sized trees (ranging from 5.1 to 8.9 inches d.b.h.), and sawtimber-sized trees (all trees greater than 9.0 inches d.b.h.). The most common tree species on the forest is grand fir (see "Common and Scientific Names" section); 32 percent of all trees (1.0 inch d.b.h. and larger) are grand fir trees. The next most numerous tree species are lodgepole pine and Douglas-fir at 24 and 15 percent, respectively, of all trees greater than 1.0 inch d.b.h. All other tree species each account for less then 10 percent of the total tree count. By size, sapling-sized trees are the most numerous at 66 percent of all trees greater than 1.0 inch d.b.h. Poletimber and sawtimber-sized tree counts are fairly equally divided at 16 percent and 17 percent, respectively. The species that have the majority (58 percent) of larger sawtimber-sized trees are grand fir (30 percent) and Douglas-fir (28 percent).

The most common tree species on the forest is grand fir.

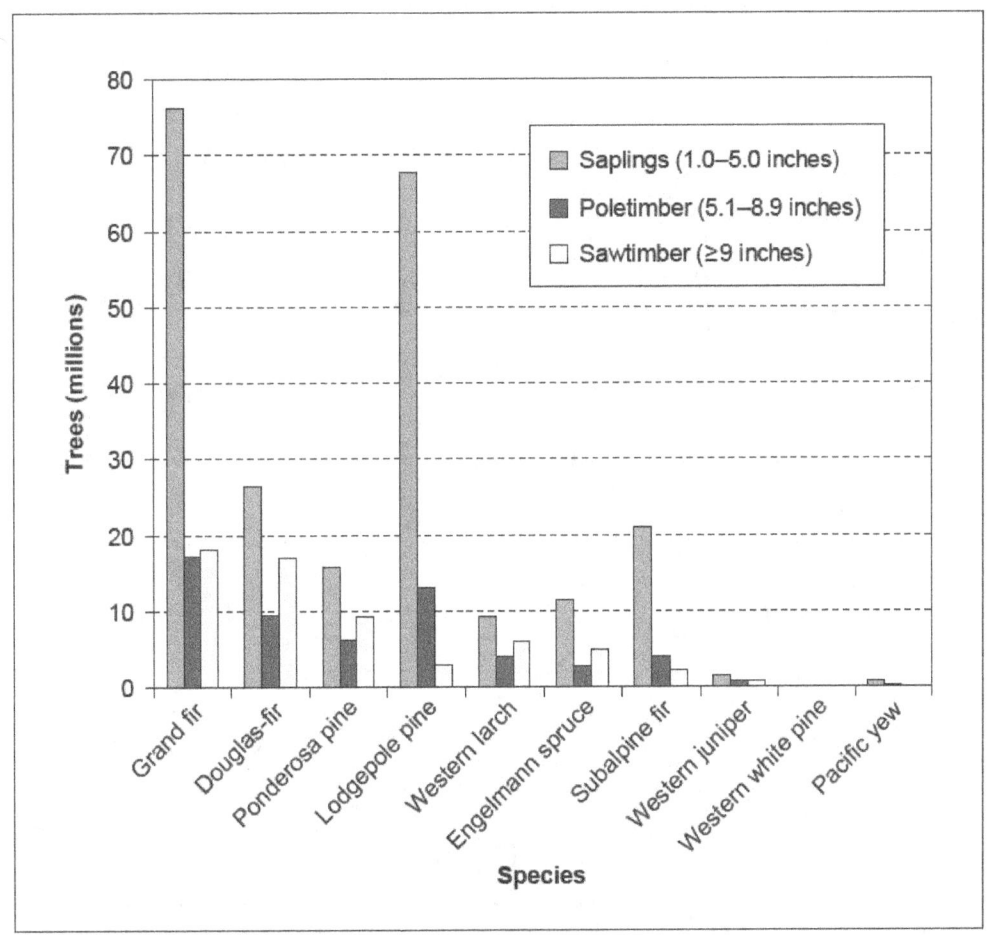

Figure 7—Number of trees by species, Umatilla National Forest, 2002 (occasion 2 data only).

Basal Area

Tree count provides an estimate of how numerous trees are across the entire national forest, but it does not provide a good representation of the distribution or density of these trees for any "typical" acre of forest land. Basal area is the cross-sectional area of a single tree stem (including bark) at the point of diameter measurement (d.b.h. in this case), but it is usually expressed as the sum of the cross-sectional area for all stems in a tree stand in square feet per acre. Figure 8 shows average basal area by forest type. Engelmann spruce and grand fir are the two forest types with the greatest tree densities when expressed as average basal area per acre. Each of these types carry more than 120 ft^2/acre of basal area on average (130 and 126 ft^2/acre, respectively). The types with the next highest average densities are Douglas-fir, western larch, and subalpine fir. Each of these types has an average basal area of between 90 and 110 ft^2/acre (Douglas-fir is 93 ft^2/acre, western larch is 91 ft^2/acre, and subalpine fir is 104 ft^2/acre). All other forest types tend to have less than 80 ft^2/acre of basal area on average.

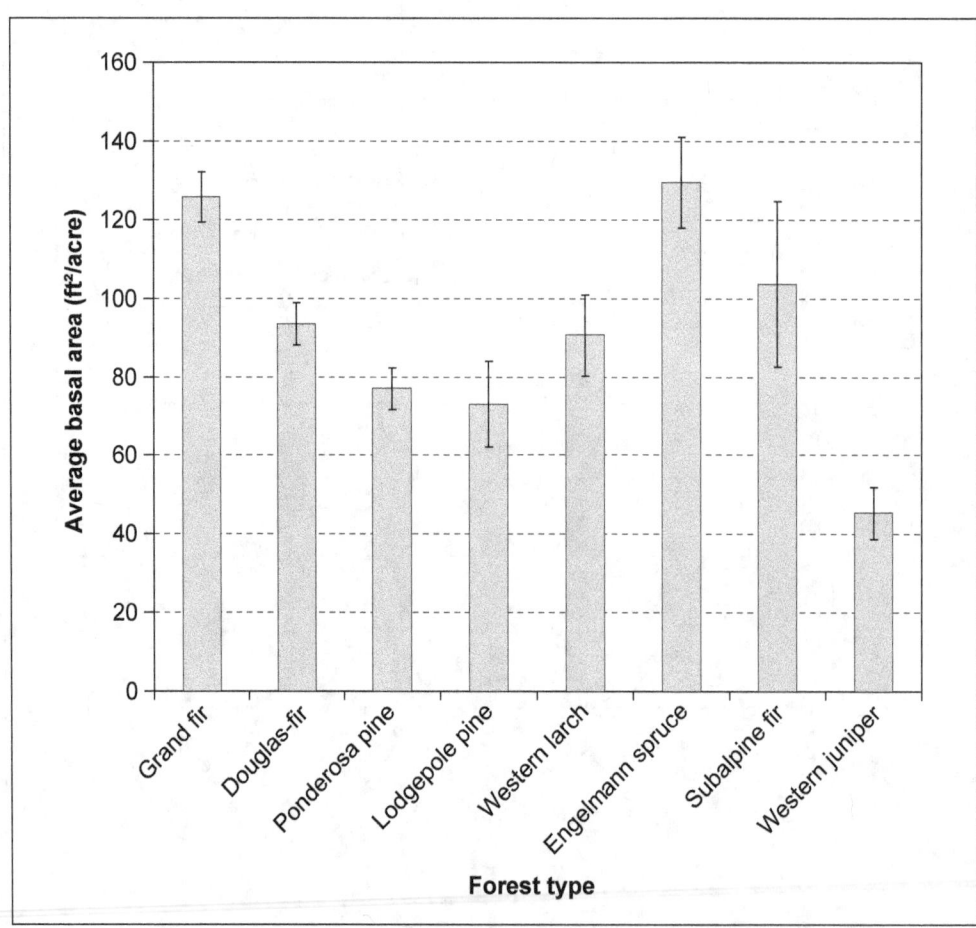

Figure 8—Average basal area by forest type with standard error of the estimate, Umatilla National Forest, 2002 (occasion 2 data only).

Stand-Size Class

The distribution of tree sizes can also be evaluated by looking at stand-size class (rather than basal area, discussed previously). Stand-size class is a classification of forest land based on the predominant diameter of live trees contributing the majority of stocking for a plot. On the UNF, small sawtimber-sized stands (9.0 to 19.0 inches d.b.h.) are predominant for 69 percent of forest-land acreage (fig. 9). Large sawtimber-sized stands (greater than 20 inches d.b.h.) occupy the next highest percentage of forest-land acreage at 21 percent. Together, seedlings and saplings (<1.0 to 5.0 inches d.b.h.) and poletimber-sized stands (5.1 to 8.0 inches d.b.h.) occupy the remaining 10 percent of forest land. By forest type, 80 percent of the small sawtimber-sized stands are classified as grand fir, Douglas-fir, or ponderosa pine. For large sawtimber-sized stands, this increases to 95 percent of the forest land being classified as grand fir, Douglas-fir, or ponderosa pine types (fig. 10).

On the Umatilla NF, small sawtimber-sized stands (9.0 to 19.0 inches d.b.h.) are predominant for 69 percent of forest-land acreage.

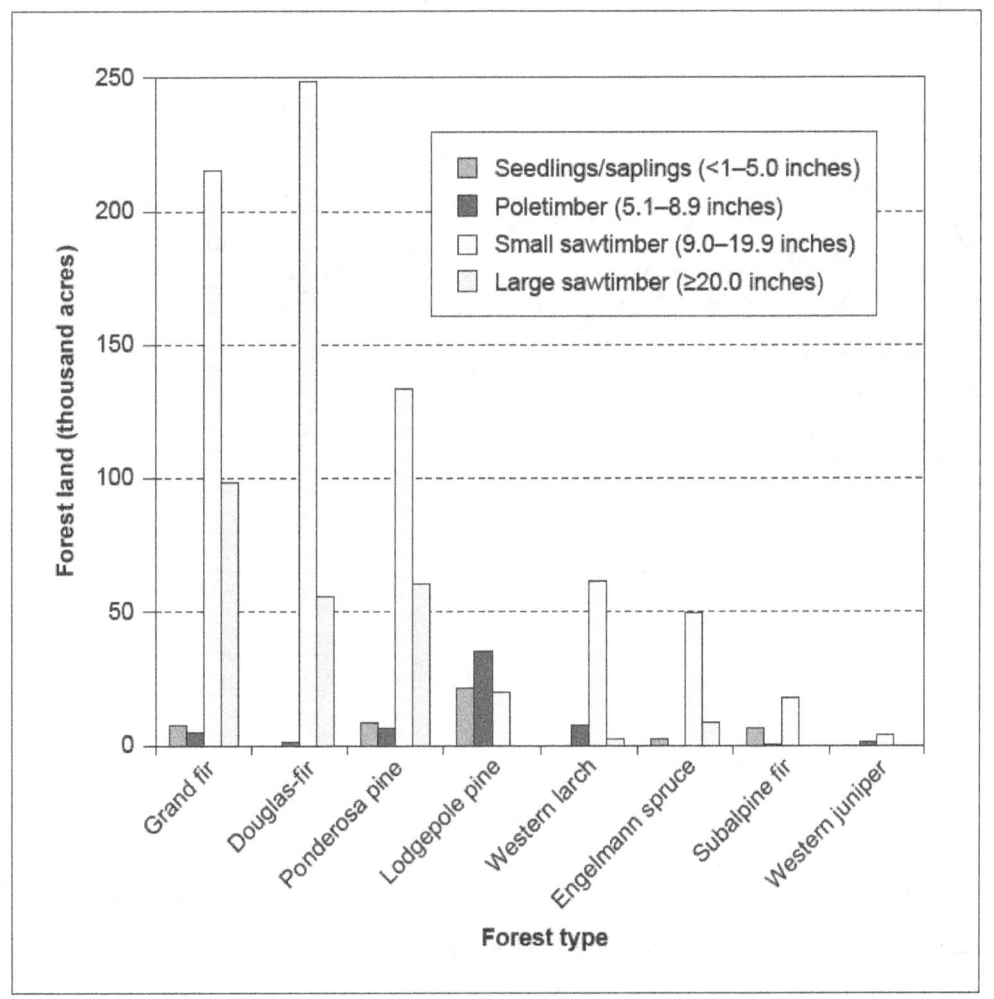

Figure 9—Forest-land area by stand-size class and forest type, Umatilla National Forest, 2002 (occasion 2 data only).

Umatilla National Forest

Figure 10—Ponderosa pine forest type, one of the three major forest types in the large sawtimber size class on the Umatilla National Forest.

Forest Health and Productivity

Biomass

The distribution and characteristics of forest biomass are necessary for the assessment of important issues such as fire behavior, carbon and nutrient cycling, soil structure, and wildlife habitat. Inventory crews sampled both standing live and dead trees within circular plots. In addition, crews sampled down (dead) logs greater than 3 inches diameter on five, 51-ft transects at each plot (fig. 11). Standing live trees, standing dead trees, and down logs contribute to the biomass and account for the total biomass in the following discussion. Dead biomass consists of standing dead trees and down logs.

Umatilla National Forest

Figure 11—Down logs in the lodgepole pine forest type; down logs were sampled on 51-ft transects on each plot.

It is not surprising that the distribution of biomass by forest type and by species on the forest is very similar to the distribution of forest-land acreage by forest type and volume by species. The forest types with the greatest biomass are the types with the most forest-land acreage: grand fir, Douglas-fir, and ponderosa pine. The grand fir forest type alone accounts for 38 percent of the total standing live, standing dead, and down log biomass (fig. 12). Douglas-fir is the next most important forest type with 24 percent of the total biomass, and the ponderosa pine type has 12 percent of the total biomass. All other forest types combined account for less than 30 percent of the total biomass on the forest.

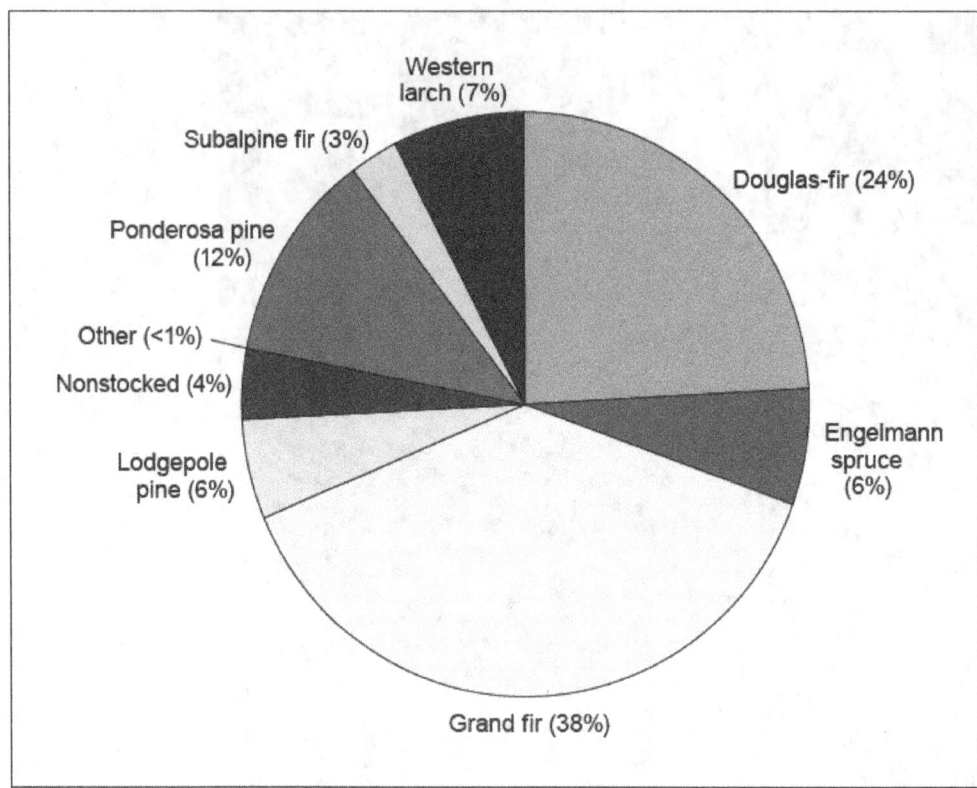

Figure 12—Distribution of total biomass by forest type, Umatilla National Forest, 1996 (occasion 1 data only).

On the Umatilla NF there are about 40.1 million tons of live standing biomass, about 11.2 million tons of standing dead biomass, and about 9.1 million tons of down log biomass.

Table 3 provides total standing live, standing dead, and down log biomass in dry tons along with the associated standard error of each estimate. On the UNF there are about 40.1 million tons of live standing biomass, about 11.2 million tons of standing dead biomass, and about 9.1 million tons of down log biomass.

Engelmann spruce, grand fir, and western larch forest types were found to have the greatest average total biomass with over 60 tons per acre (fig. 13). Ponderosa pine forests typically had just over 30 tons per acre. Douglas-fir, lodgepole pine, and subalpine fir had intermediate amounts of biomass. With standing live tree biomass being the largest component of total biomass in all forest types, it is not surprising that the distribution of total biomass by forest type closely matches the distribution of volume by forest type. Ponderosa pine and Douglas-fir forest types have the lowest dead biomass to live biomass ratios at about 30 percent, while western larch, lodgepole pine, and nonstocked types have ratios over 80 percent.

The greatest amounts of dead biomass per acre (standing and down wood combined) were found in the Engelmann spruce, grand fir, lodgepole pine, and western larch forest types with over 23 tons per acre (fig. 13). The Douglas-fir, nonstocked, and ponderosa pine types had less than half the above value. Overall, standing dead

Table 3—Total standing live, dead, and down log biomass by forest type, Umatilla National Forest, 1996 (occasion 1 data only)

Forest type	Standing live		Standing dead		Down logs	
	Total	SE(%)	Total	SE(%)	Total	SE(%)
	Thousand tons					
Grand fir	14,999	1,700 (11)	4,904	600 (12)	3,106	351 (11)
Douglas-fir	11,104	1,123 (10)	2,045	393 (19)	1,456	175 (12)
Ponderosa pine	5,284	745 (14)	876	219 (25)	915	158 (17)
Lodgepole pine	1,725	347 (20)	673	164 (24)	1,033	284 (27)
Western larch	2,480	564 (23)	1,188	448 (38)	836	240 (29)
Engelmann spruce	2,481	540 (22)	565	158 (28)	792	166 (21)
Subalpine fir	1,121	288 (26)	214	61 (29)	287	72 (25)
Other	64	28 (44)	6	4 (67)	2	1 (50)
Nonstocked	862	111 (13)	766	226 (30)	635	111 (17)
Total	40,120	1,615 (4)	11,237	770 (7)	9,062	507 (6)

SE = standard error.

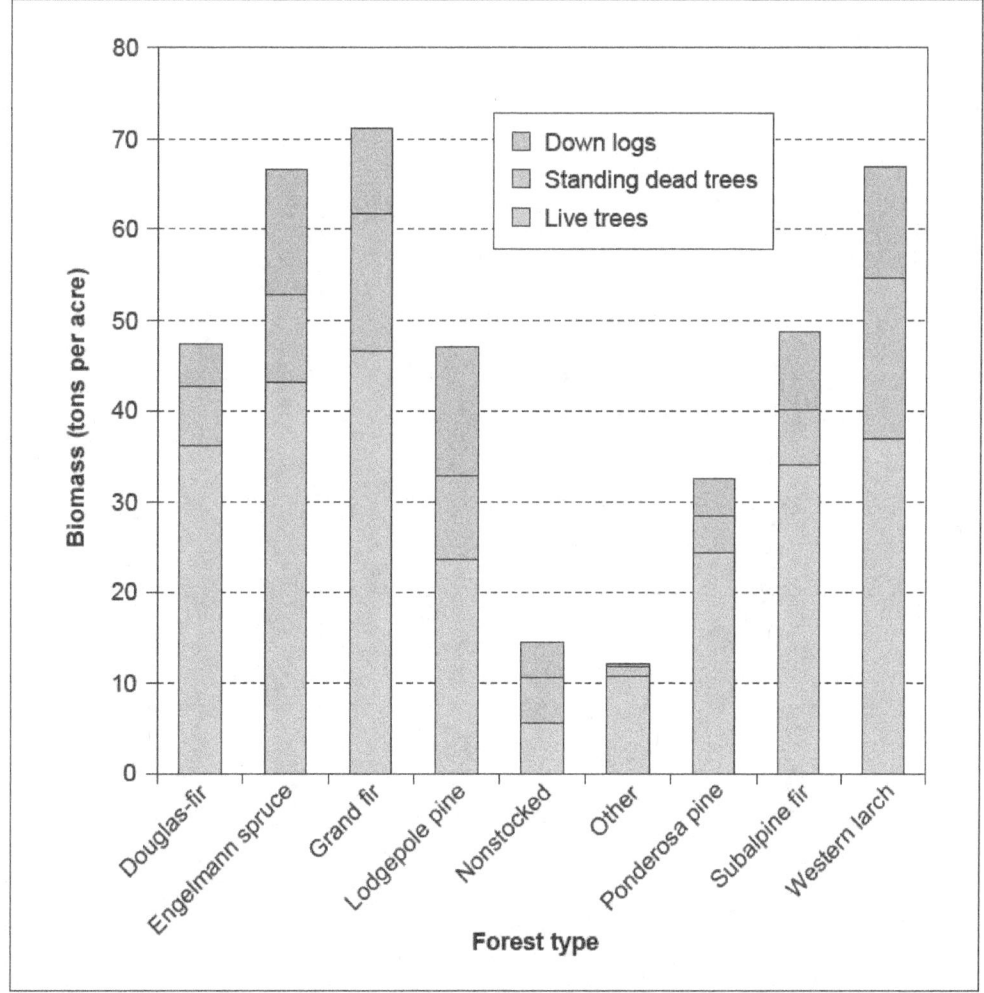

Figure 13—Average weight of live and dead biomass by forest type, Umatilla National Forest, 1996 (occasion 1 data only).

tree biomass tended to be greater than down log biomass (9.0 tons per acre versus 7.3 tons per acre on average).

When analyzed by stand size, total biomass per acre is found to be higher in the larger stand size classes (fig. 14). The proportion of live biomass to dead biomass also increases in the larger stand sizes. The seedling-sapling and poletimber size classes have the largest per-acre values for down log biomass (12.8 and 10.8 tons per acre, respectively). This result probably reflects the result of historical disturbance processes where most of the previous tree cohort was killed and then fell over, and a new tree cohort became established and is now in the seedling, sapling, or pole size class (fig. 15).

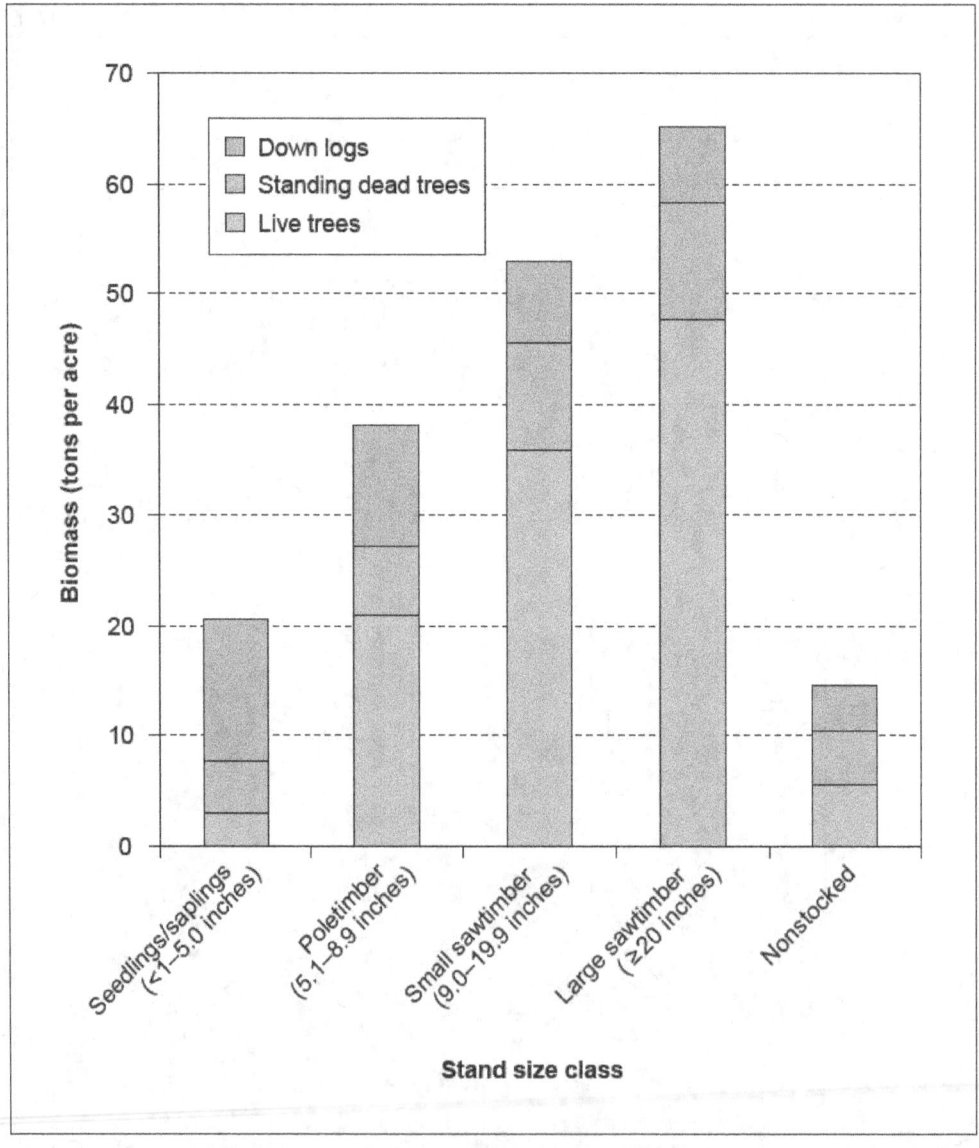

Figure 14—Average biomass tons per acre by stand size, Umatilla National Forest, 1996 (occasion 1 data only).

Umatilla National Forest

Figure 15—A new tree cohort of lodgepole pine getting established after a stand-replacing disturbance event.

The current total net volume of wood in live trees on the forest is estimated to be in excess of 14.0 billion board feet.

Wood Volume

The current total net volume of wood in live trees on the forest is estimated to be in excess of 14.0 billion board feet (±6 percent SE). This includes all live trees on forest land of sawtimber size. Sawtimber is defined as softwood species 9.0 inches d.b.h. and larger, and hardwood species 11.0 inches d.b.h. and larger. Table 4 is a breakdown of volume by species for both first and second occasions.

As was the case for forest type (fig. 5), the majority of volume comes from three species: grand fir, Douglas-fir, and ponderosa pine. These three forest types occupy 68 percent of the forest land. By species, grand fir, Douglas-fir, and ponderosa pine contribute 76 percent of the total board-foot volume (fig. 16). The next two important species are western larch and Engelmann spruce, contributing 11 percent

Table 4—Forest land live tree timber volume by species and measurement occasion, Umatilla National Forest, 1996 and 2002 (occasions 1 and 2)

Species	Occasion 1				Occasion 2			
	Total	SE (%)	Total	SE (%)	Total	SE (%)	Total	SE (%)
	Million board feet		*Million cubic feet*		*Million board feet*		*Million cubic feet*	
Grand fir	4,854	468 (10)	907	82 (9)	4,622	518 (11)	860	91 (11)
Douglas-fir	3,399	257 (8)	688	49 (7)	3,334	288 (9)	678	56 (8)
Ponderosa pine	2,342	219 (9)	438	38 (9)	2,773	282 (10)	517	50 (10)
Lodgepole pine	256	43 (17)	62	10 (16)	233	63 (27)	56	14 (25)
Western larch	1,378	140 (10)	268	27 (10)	1,505	203 (13)	291	38 (13)
Engelmann spruce	1,270	172 (14)	237	31 (13)	1,354	231 (17)	255	43 (17)
Subalpine fir	369	64 (17)	81	14 (17)	232	66 (28)	51	14 (27)
Western white pine	3	2 (67)	<1	—	2	2 (100)	<1	—
Black cottonwood	6	5 (83)	1	1 (100)	—	—	—	—
Total	13,877	681 (5)	2,682	120 (4)	14,055	775 (6)	2,708	139 (5)

SE = standard error.

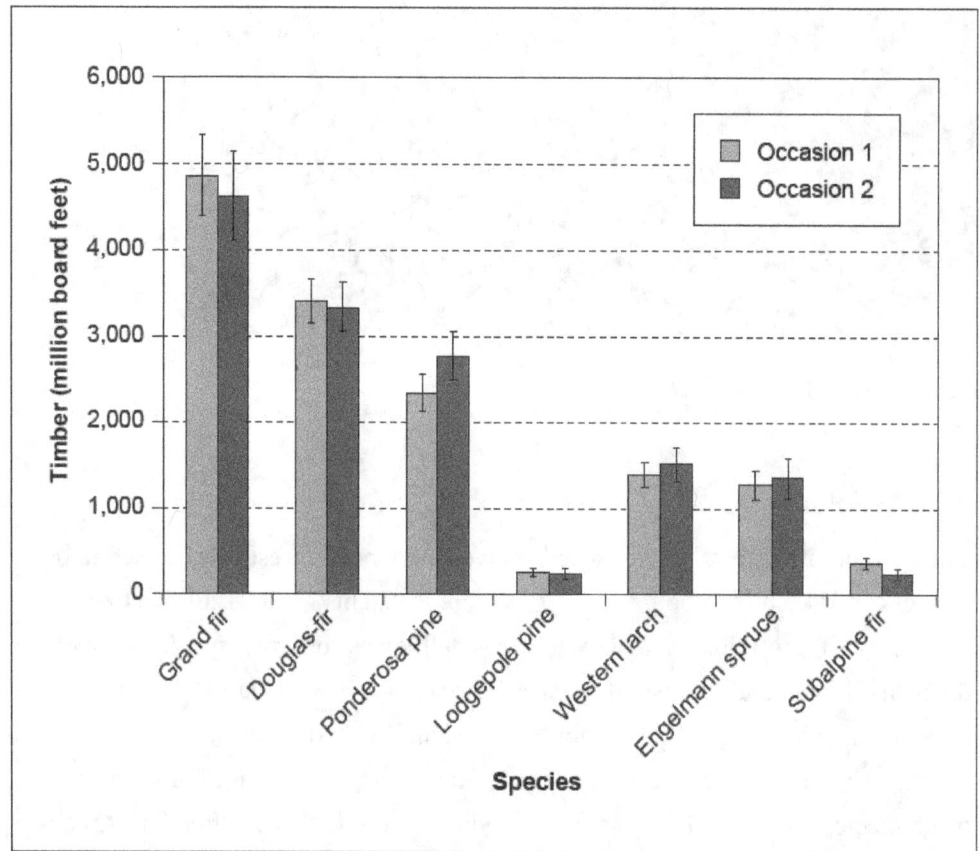

Figure 16—Forest-land live tree timber by species and measurement occasion with standard error of the estimate, Umatilla National Forest, 1996 and 2002 (occasion 1 and 2 data).

and 10 percent, respectively, to total volume (fig. 17). Lodgepole pine and subalpine fir play a minor role, each adding 2 percent to the total board-foot volume on forest land. In terms of both forest type acreage and volume by tree species, grand fir is a major species on the forest. By forest type, both grand fir and Douglas-fir each occupy about 25 percent of the forest land.

Umatilla National Forest

Figure 17—Engelmann spruce forest type. Engelmann spruce is a minor forest type, and it contributes about 10 percent of the Umatilla National Forest's total board-foot timber volume.

Looking at live tree volume by species, grand fir accounts for 33 percent of the sawtimber volume, whereas Douglas-fir accounts for 24 percent of the sawtimber volume. This suggests that not only is grand fir an important forest type but, as a species, it is occurring in many other forest types where it is not the majority species. There is no significant difference in board-foot volume by species between occasions when looking at all forest land on the forest (fig. 16).

In addition to understanding where the volume on the forest comes from by tree species, it is important to evaluate volume distribution by diameter class. Figure 18 shows the percentage of total net cubic foot volume (gross cubic foot volume minus defect deductions) on forest land by diameter class; it illustrates that most of

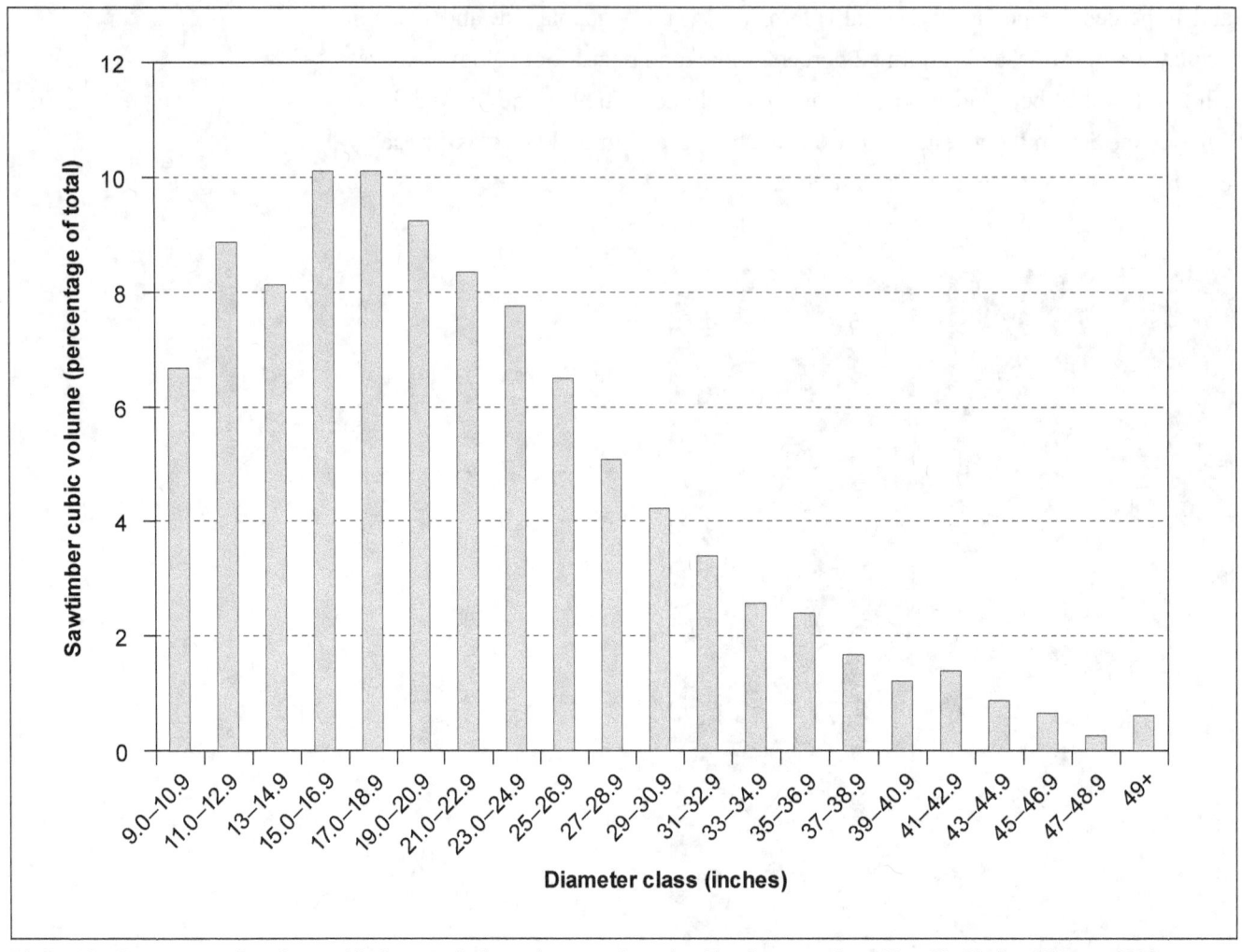

Figure 18—Percentage of total net cubic foot sawtimber volume on forest land by diameter class, Umatilla National Forest, 2002 (occasion 2 data only).

the live tree volume is in smaller trees and that the contribution by diameter class tends to decline for trees larger than about 19.0 inches d.b.h. In fact, the majority of net volume comes from trees 11 to 23 inches d.b.h. These trees constitute approximately 55 percent of the total volume. Only about 5 percent of the total volume is from the largest trees (those larger than 40.0 inches d.b.h.).

Snags and Down Logs

The distribution and condition of standing dead trees (snags) are especially important to many bird species for nesting, roosting, and foraging. Down logs are also important for foraging and cover for many birds and mammals (Bull et al. 1997). In the context of wildlife habitat, the distribution, condition, and size of individual logs and snags is more important than the total biomass or volume of dead wood (snags and logs).

Figure 19—Young grand fir trees growing up through a mature western larch forest (dark stems) containing abundant snags.

The western larch and lodgepole pine forest types were found to have the most snags per acre.

The western larch and lodgepole pine forest types were found to have the most snags per acre (fig. 19), but these snags also tended to be in the smaller diameter classes (fig. 20). The snags considered most useful for cavity-nesting birds are those greater than 20 inches d.b.h. (Bull et al. 1997). Overall, forest-land acreage averaged 2.7 snags greater than 20 inches d.b.h. per acre. Within the grand fir forest type, snags this size averaged 5 per acre with only 1 per acre in the "recent" decay class.

On average there were 3.7 logs greater than 20 inches d.b.h. per acre on forest land (fig. 21). Within the grand fir forest type, there were about 5 logs per acre this size. The lodgepole pine type averaged just one log larger than 20 inches d.b.h. per acre. Overall, forest land averaged 288 down logs per acre (all diameter classes).

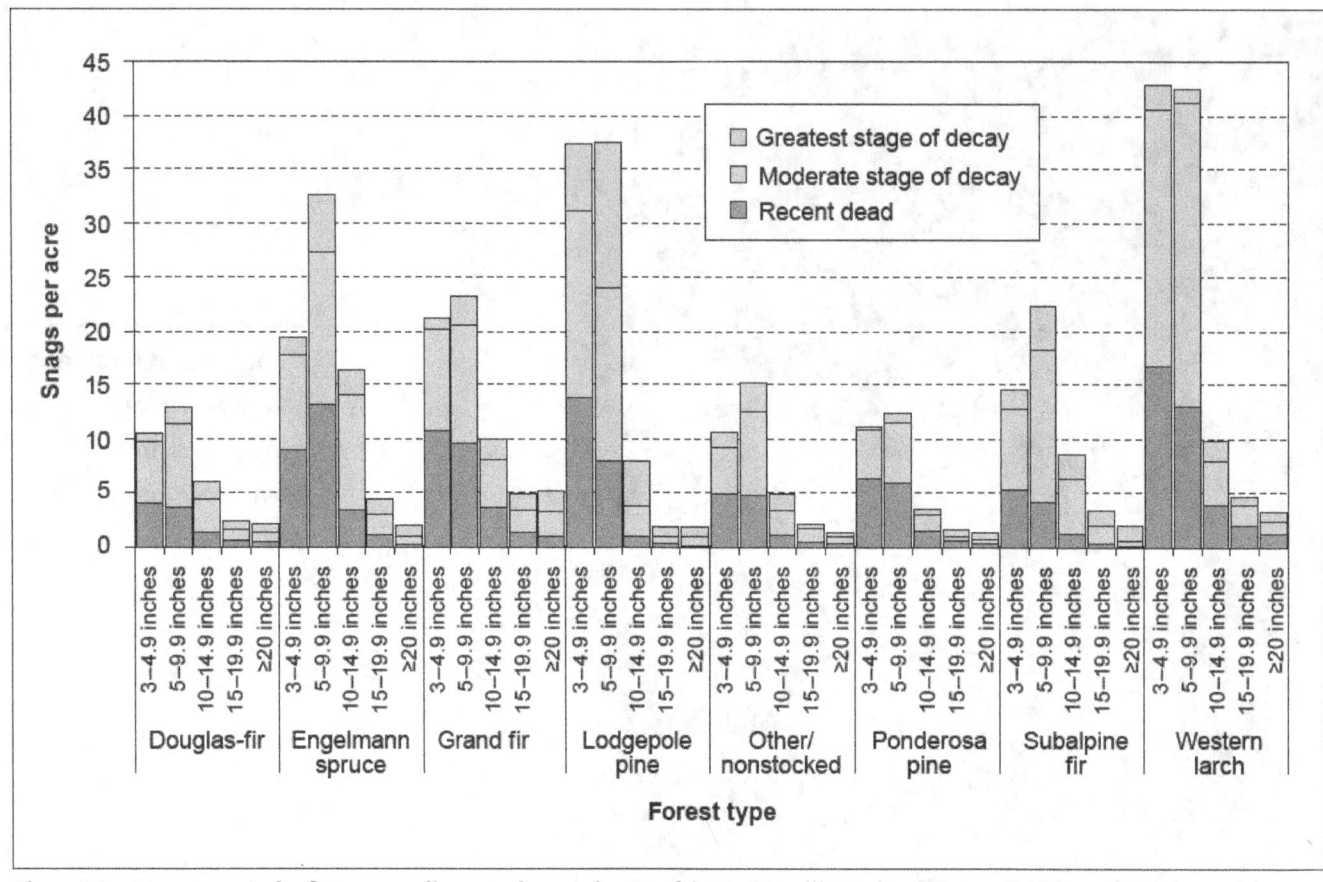

Figure 20—Snags per acre by forest type, diameter class, and stage of decay, Umatilla National Forest, 1996 (occasion 1 data only).

Although we cannot directly assess mortality before the first plot installations, measurement of standing dead trees at the time of plot installation can provide some insight about past mortality events. When standing dead trees were measured, inventory crews assigned each tree a "decay class" describing its stage of decomposition (Thomas et al. 1979). Trees in the first class generally have intact bark and limbs and have little decay of the bole. Trees in the second class will be losing limbs and bark and may have advanced decay of heartwood. Trees in the third through fifth categories have lost most of their bark and limbs and have progressively more decay and loss of the bole's original form. Snags in the highest stages of decay are relatively uncommon, so for this report we have combined classes three through five. Snags in the first class are assumed to be relatively recent mortality, probably dying within the previous 5 years before plot measurement.

Overall, 36 percent of all snags sampled during the first occasion were assigned to the first decay class and are considered to have died within the previous 5 years. As can be seen in figure 22, the species with the highest proportion of snags in the recent mortality category are Douglas-fir and grand fir (41 and 45 percent,

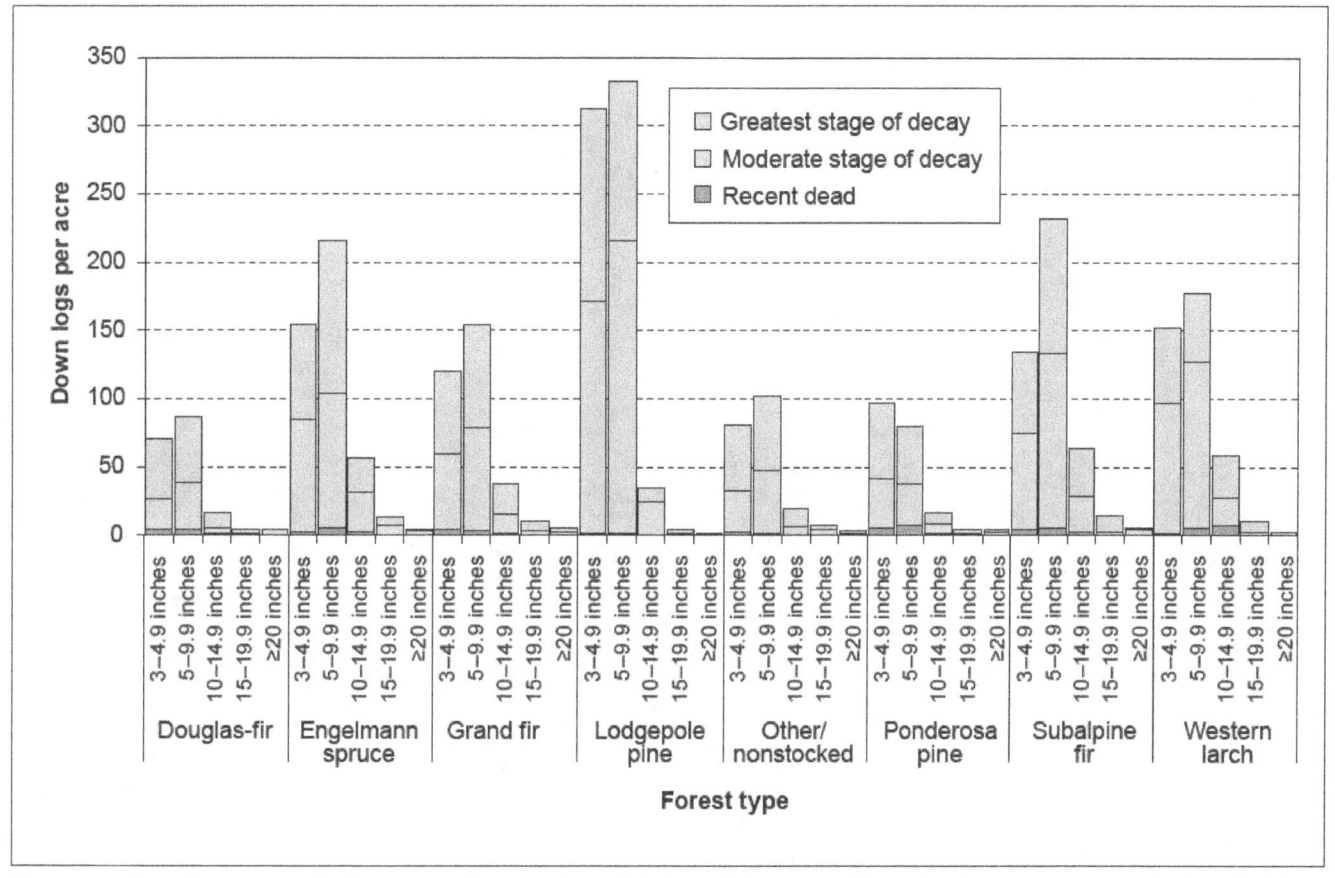

Figure 21—Down logs per acre by forest type, diameter class, and stage of decay, Umatilla National Forest, 1996 (occasion 1 data only).

respectively). All other species averaged 29 percent of their snags being classified as recent mortality. A pulse of Douglas-fir and grand fir mortality in the late 1980s and early 1990s would coincide with an outbreak of western spruce budworm (*Choristoneura occidentalis* Freeman) in northeastern Oregon (Powell 1994, Wickman 1992). Figure 23 shows areas where aerial survey reconnaissance flights detected spruce budworm defoliation between 1986 and 1992 where host trees had top-kill or complete defoliation. It should not be assumed that all defoliated trees within these areas died, but it is likely that many did die either directly from defoliation or were stressed to the point of succumbing to other insects or disease.

Insects and Disease

The actions of insects, diseases, and fire have always had a role in determining the condition of forest land in the Western United States (Sampson and Adams 1994). The remeasurement of plots across the UNF provides an opportunity to directly assess their impact over a 4- to 8-year period. Where trees that were alive at the first plot installation were found to be dead at the time of remeasurement, inventory

A pulse of Douglas-fir and grand fir mortality in the late 1980s and early 1990s would coincide with an outbreak of western spruce budworm (*Choristoneura occidentalis* Freeman) in northeastern Oregon.

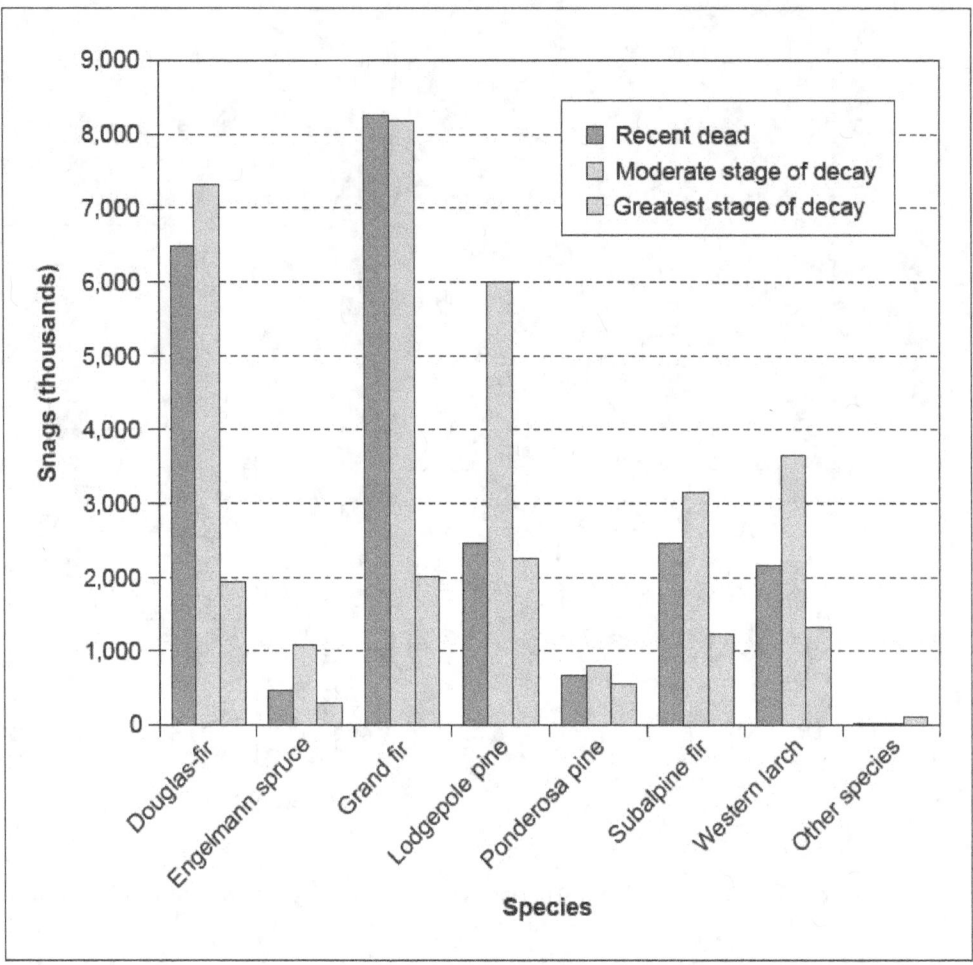

Figure 22—Number of snags by species and decay class, Umatilla National Forest, 1996 (occasion 1 data only).

crews attempted to determine the reason for tree death. It was possible to determine the causes of death for trees on the 326 remeasured plots of panels A and D.

The most commonly recorded cause of death was bark beetle attack, with over half of the mortality volume attributed to these insects that feed on the cambium of living trees (fig. 24). Slightly more than one quarter of the mortality volume was attributed to trees that had fallen or been physically damaged. In addition to trees that were blown over during windstorms, this group likely includes those trees that had been killed by insects or diseases, but the exact cause of death could not be determined at the time of remeasurement. The remaining 18 percent of mortality was attributed to other insects, diseases, and fire.[3]

---

[3] Determining cause of death is difficult owing to a lapse of time between tree death and observation by a field crew, and often more than one mortality agent is involved. Thus, these data should be used with other sources such as an aerial survey for a more accurate assessment of cause of death.

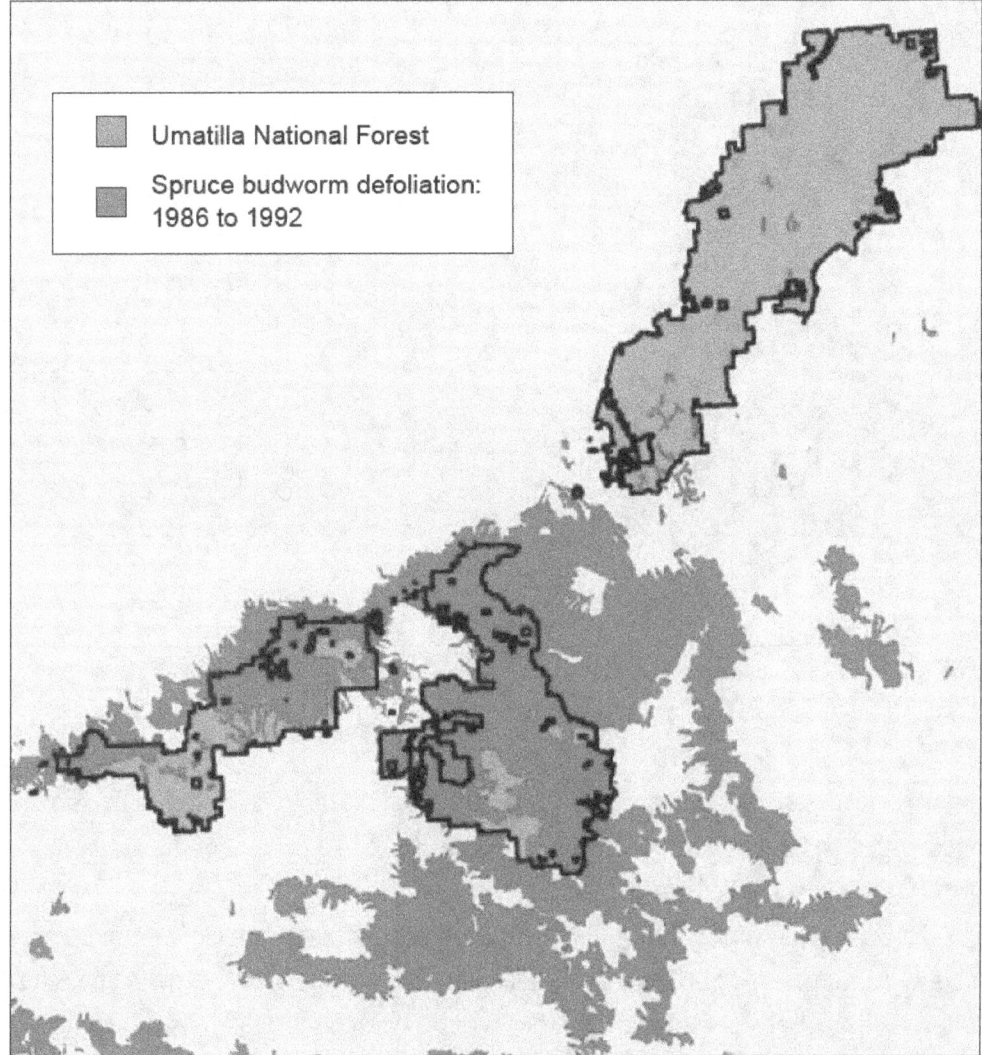

Figure 23—Areas of spruce budworm defoliation detected by aerial survey, Umatilla National Forest, 1986–1992 (source: Oregon Department of Forestry, Washington Department of Natural Resources, USDA Forest Service-Forest Health Protection Cooperative Annual Aerial Survey).

Tree stands weakened by successive years of budworm feeding are more susceptible to bark beetle attack.

Much of the bark beetle impact was related to a wide-ranging outbreak of western spruce budworm, a defoliating insect that primarily feeds on the foliage of grand fir and Douglas-fir (with lesser amounts of feeding on Engelmann spruce, subalpine fir, and western larch). Between 1980 and 1992, millions of acres in the Blue Mountains were affected by budworm defoliation. Tree stands weakened by successive years of budworm feeding are more susceptible to bark beetle attack. This situation commonly occurred on the southern half of the UNF (and south of there on the Malheur National Forest as well) (Powell 1994).

Although root disease was recorded as a cause of death for only 2 percent of the volume, root disease is common on the forest and likely predisposes trees to attack

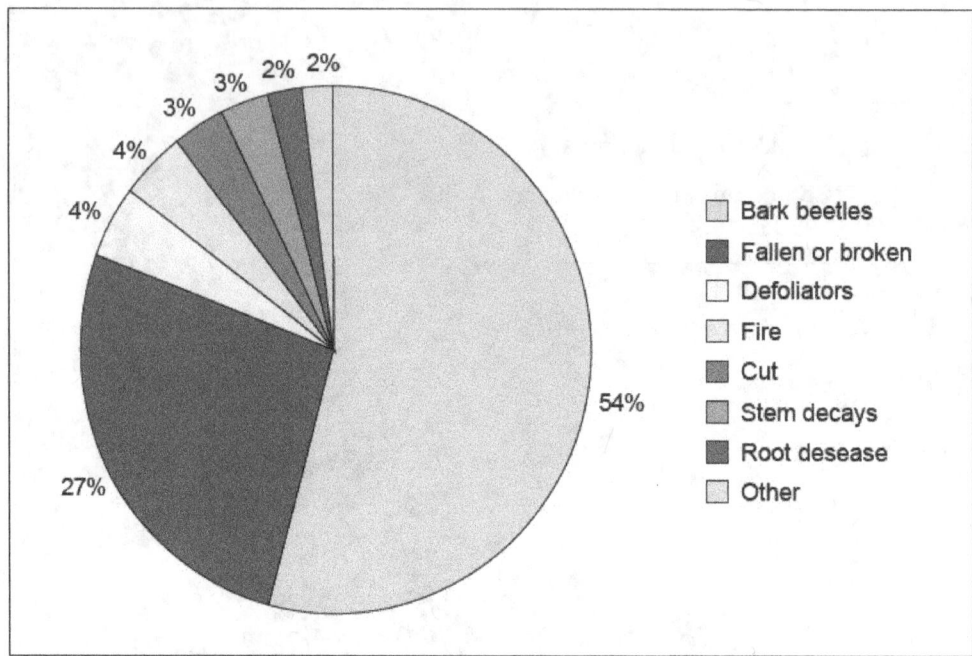

Figure 24—Percentage of total mortality volume by cause of death, Umatilla National Forest, 1996 (occasion 1 data only).

by bark beetles and other insects or diseases.[4] Root disease was found to be associated with 8 percent of the forest land overall, and with 12 percent of the grand fir forest type specifically (fig. 25).

How is the presence of root disease related to bark beetle attack? Figure 26 shows the percentage of trees ≥ 5-inches d.b.h. killed by bark beetles with and without root disease present. In grand fir, bark beetle-caused mortality appears to be higher when root disease was present. In other species, the difference is minor. The results displayed in figure 26 indicate that root disease might be predisposing grand fir stands to attack by bark beetles (fir engraver; *Scolytus ventralis* LeConte). A similar situation has been observed for Douglas-fir dwarf mistletoe (*Arceuthobium douglasii* Engelmann) and western spruce budworm in Douglas-fir stands: dwarf mistletoe parasitism was apparently predisposing Douglas-fir trees to budworm-caused mortality during the 1980–92 budworm outbreak (Powell 1994).

---

[4] In addition to recording the occurrence of root disease on individual trees, inventory crews searched for root disease at each forested subplot and recorded its presence if found within 50 ft of the subplot center. For the purposes of this report, we assume that a subplot with root disease within 50 ft of subplot center will have its area influenced by the disease.

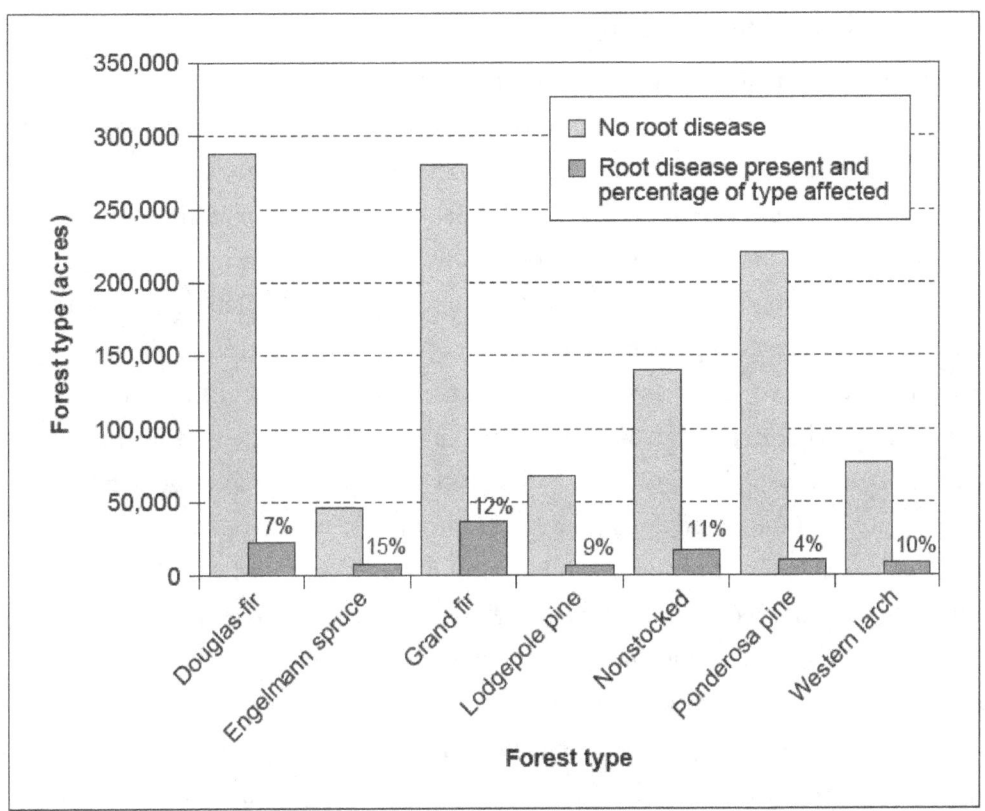

Figure 25—Area associated with root disease by forest type, Umatilla National Forest, 1996 (occasion 1 data only).

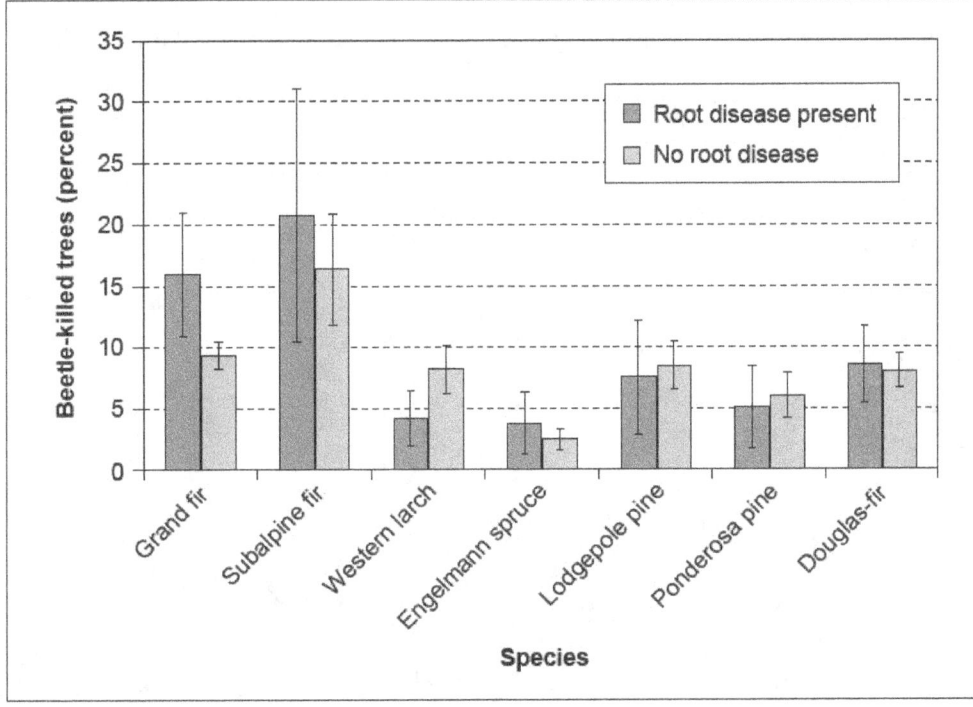

Figure 26—Bark beetle mortality with and without root disease present with standard error of the estimate, Umatilla National Forest, 1996 (occasion 1 data only).

Wildfire Risk Assessment

Several different models have been developed that allow an assessment of wildfire risk. For this analysis, we used the Fire and Fuels Extension (FFE) model (Reinhardt and Crookston 2003) to the Forest Vegetation Simulator (FVS) growth and yield model (USDA Forest Service 2005). All plot data from the first measurement occasion is used for estimates of fire risk with the Blue Mountain variant of the FVS-FFE model. We used first-occasion data, as all plot measurements including dead wood are available for modeling. To estimate wildfire risk, we use torching index and crowning index, two variables that have been used in recently published studies as a measure of wildfire risk (Fiedler and others 2004, Fried and others 2005, Scott and Reinhardt 2001). Torching index is the 20-ft windspeed (the average windspeed in miles per hour measured at 20 ft above the ground) at which a surface fire is expected to ignite the crown layer, and crowning index is the 20-ft windspeed (in miles per hour) needed to support an actively spreading crown fire (Reinhardt and Crookston 2003). The stands that are at greatest risk of torching are those with a torching index of about 20 miles per hour (mph) or less.

Within the subalpine fir and Engelmann spruce forest types, more than half of the area (64 percent for subalpine fir and 61 percent for Engelmann spruce) has a torching index that is less than 20 mph (fig. 27). The large proportion of area at high risk of torching within these types is likely due to lower crown base heights that create more opportunity for surface fires to ignite ladder fuels, allowing the fire to move up into the crown. For all forest-land area, 43 percent is at risk of a wildfire torching.

Within the subalpine fir and Engelmann spruce forest types, more than half of the area has a torching index that is less than 20 mph.

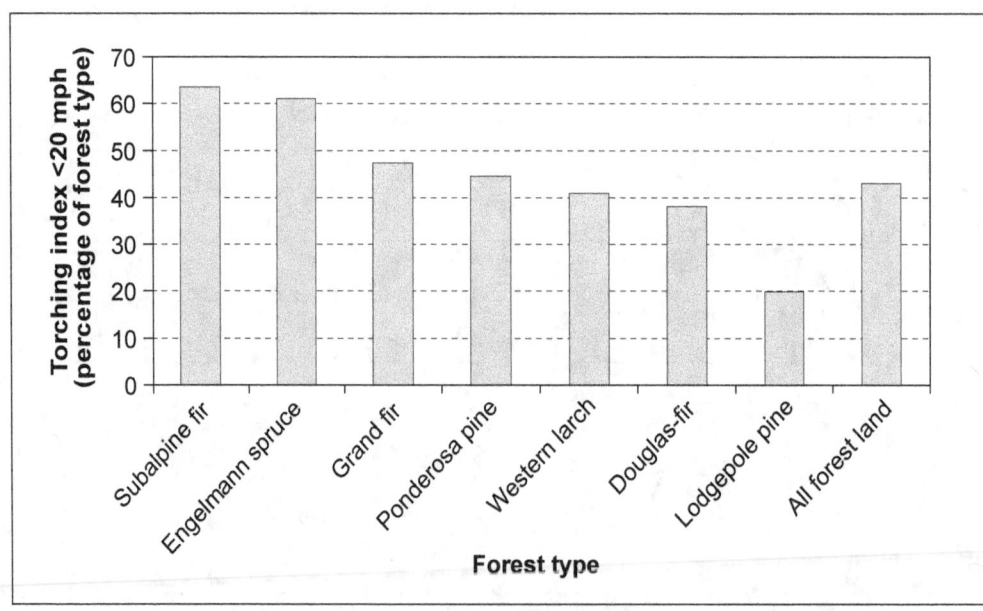

Figure 27—Percentage of area with a torching index less than 20 miles per hour, by forest type, as predicted by the FVS-FFE model, Umatilla National Forest, 1996 (occasion 1 data only).

Figure 28 shows the percentage of area with a crowning index less than 20 mph by forest type. As with torching index, those stands that have a crowning index of 20 mph or less tend to be at the highest risk of an active crown fire. On the UNF, the forest type with the greatest percentage of acres that pose the highest risk for this type of wildfire is grand fir; 34 percent of the plots classified as grand fir forest type may be at risk of an active crown fire. For all forest land, 19 percent is at risk of a wildfire crowning (fig. 29).

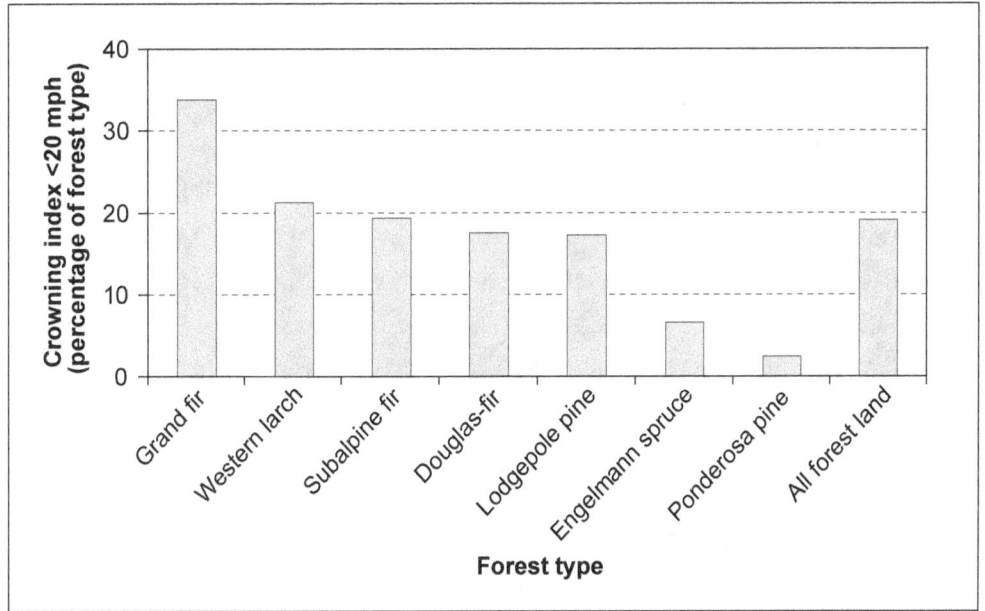

Figure 28—Percentage of area with a crowning index less than 20 miles per hour, by forest type, as predicted by the FVS-FFE model, Umatilla National Forest, 1996 (occasion 1 data only).

Figure 29—Aftermath of a crown fire on the southern Umatilla National Forest.

Canopy bulk density (CBD) is another way to assess crown fire potential. The CBD is the mass of available canopy fuel per unit of canopy volume (Scott and Reinhardt 2001). It is usually expressed in kilograms per cubic meter and can range from zero where there is no canopy, to about 0.4 kg/m^3 (0.025 lb/ft^3) (Powell 2005). Powell (2005) provided three categories of crown fire potential based on a range of CBD values expressed as kilograms of canopy fuel (foliage and small branches) per cubic meter of canopy volume. With low CDB (<0.05 kg/m^3 or 0.0031 lb/ft^3), crown fire is impossible or unlikely; with high CBD (>0.10 kg/m^3 or 0.0062 lb/ft^3), a crown fire can be sustained; moderate (0.05 to 0.10 kg/m^3 or 0.0031 to 0.0062 lb/ft^3) CBD values occur between the upper and lower thresholds (Powell 2005).

Simulation output from the FFE model includes estimates of CBD. Figure 30 shows canopy fuel loading risk (as defined by CBD categories) by forest type. For the UNF, the forest type with the highest acreage at potential risk for a crown fire is grand fir (120,000 acres) followed by Douglas-fir (50,000 acres). There is a large acreage now classified with "moderate" crown fire risk in the grand fir, Douglas-fir, and ponderosa pine types (361,000 acres, 29 percent of forest land). Some of these acres may move into the "high" risk category as CBD increases over time.

The forest type with the highest acreage at potential risk for a crown fire is grand fir (120,000 acres).

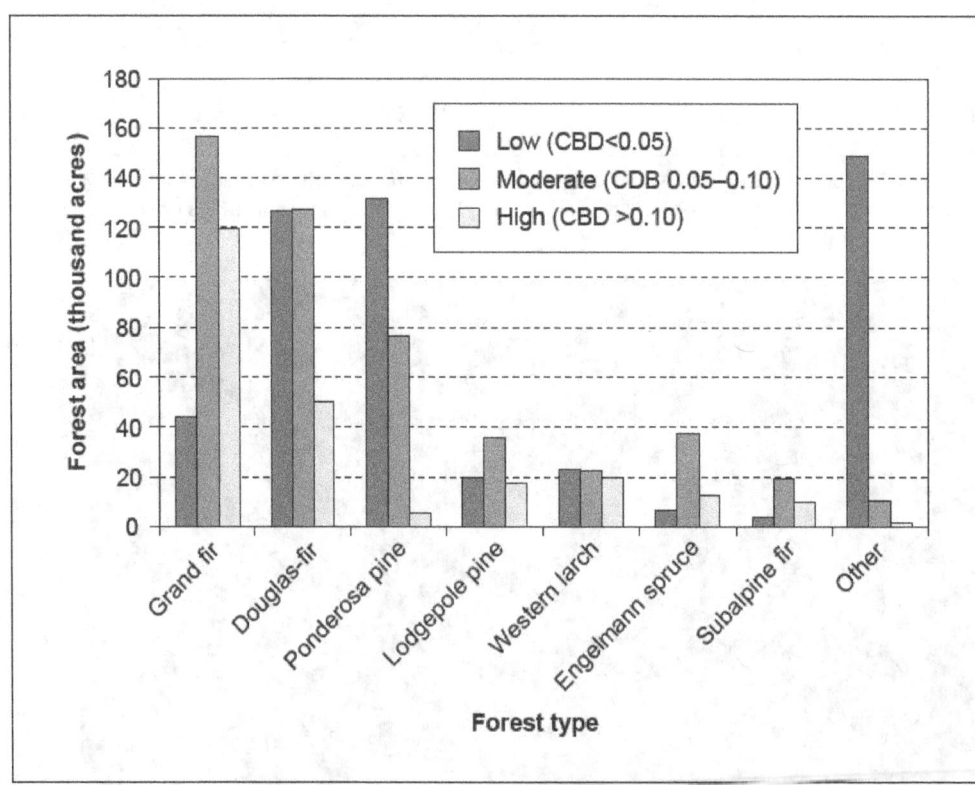

Figure 30—Canopy bulk density (CBD) by forest type as predicted by the FVS-FFE model, Umatilla National Forest, 1996 (occasion 1 data only).

Forest Growth and Mortality

Trees with about 490 million cubic feet of volume died between the first and second plot measurements, balanced by 449 million cubic feet of gross growth.[5] There is no statistically significant overall difference between mortality volume and gross growth volume. However, subalpine fir was found to have a mortality rate much higher than its growth rate. Conversely, ponderosa pine was found to be growing faster than it was dying (figs. 31 and 32). Figure 31 shows the relative cubic volumes of annual mortality and gross volume growth by tree species. Total mortality volume is predominately grand fir (39 percent) and Douglas-fir (23 percent) (fig. 33), roughly proportional to these species' contribution to total live volume. Total gross growth is predominantly grand fir (38 percent) and Douglas-fir (23 percent). Ponderosa pine proved to be a relatively healthy species over the remeasurement period. Although ponderosa pine was 18 percent of the live volume, it accounted for only 8 percent of the mortality volume and 16 percent of the growth. Conversely, subalpine fir with 4 percent of the live volume contributed 10 percent of the mortality and only 2 percent of the growth.

Subalpine fir with 4 percent of the live volume contributed 10 percent of the mortality and only 2 percent of the growth.

---

[5] As mentioned in the "Inventory Methods and Procedures" section, mortality could be reliably assessed only on the 326 remeasured plots of panels A and D. The growth and mortality figures presented here were developed from this group of plots.

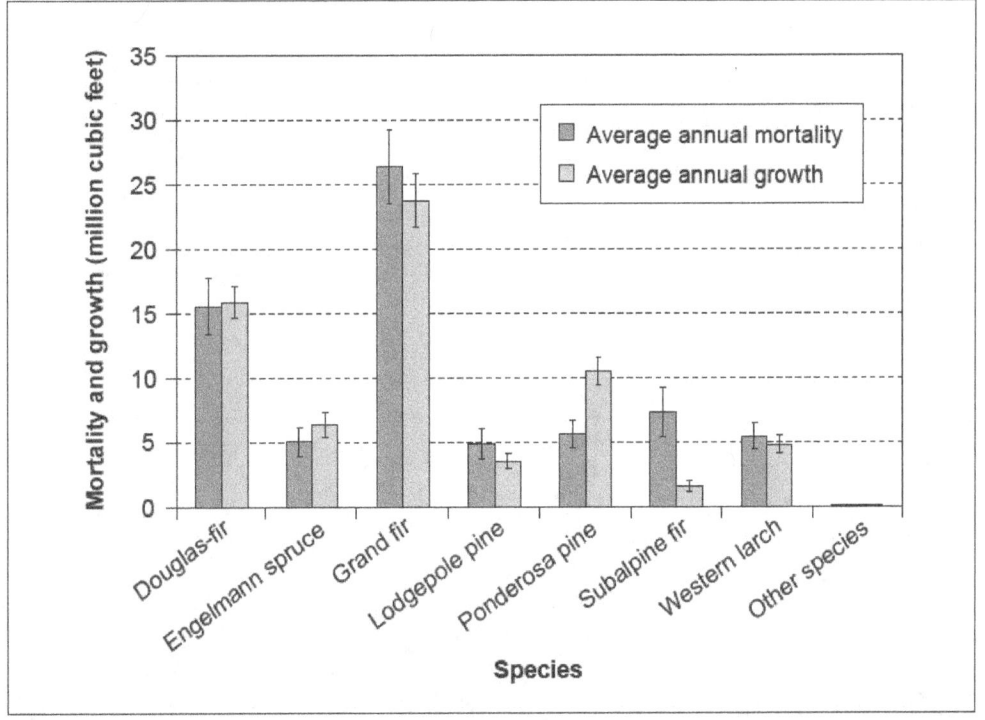

Figure 31—Average annual mortality and gross growth by species with standard error of the estimate, in millions of cubic feet for panels A and D only, Umatilla National Forest, 1996 to 2002 (occasion 1 and 2 data).

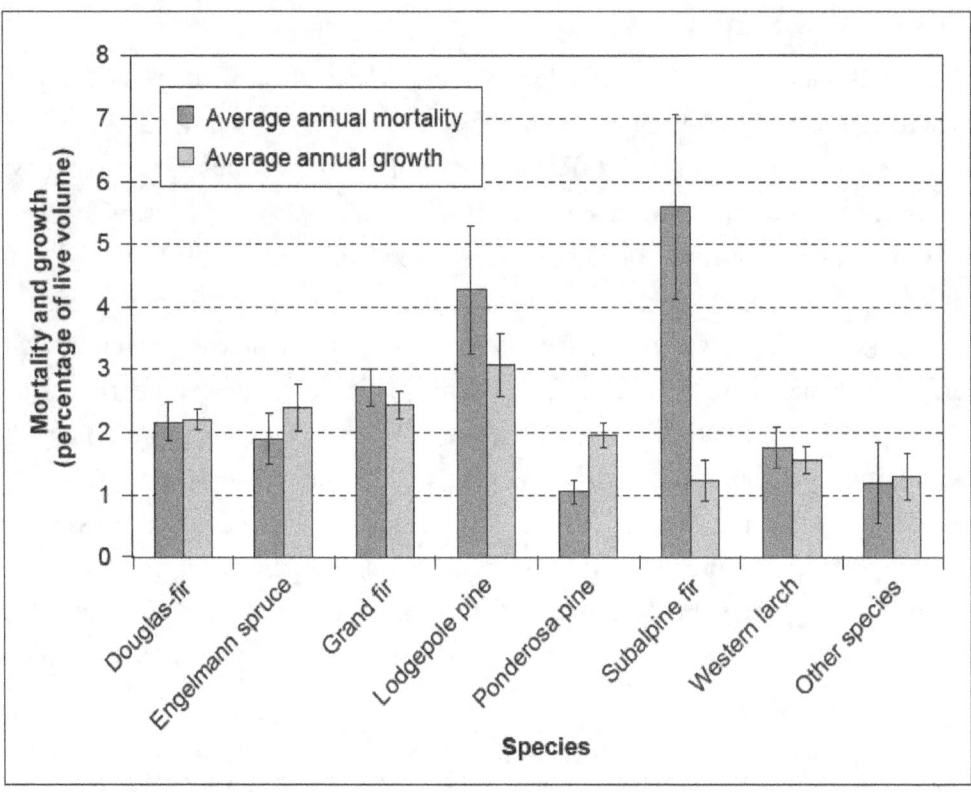

Figure 32—Average annual mortality and gross growth by species as a percentage of live cubic foot volume with standard error of the estimate, for panels A and D only, Umatilla National Forest, 1996 to 2002 (occasion 1 and 2 data).

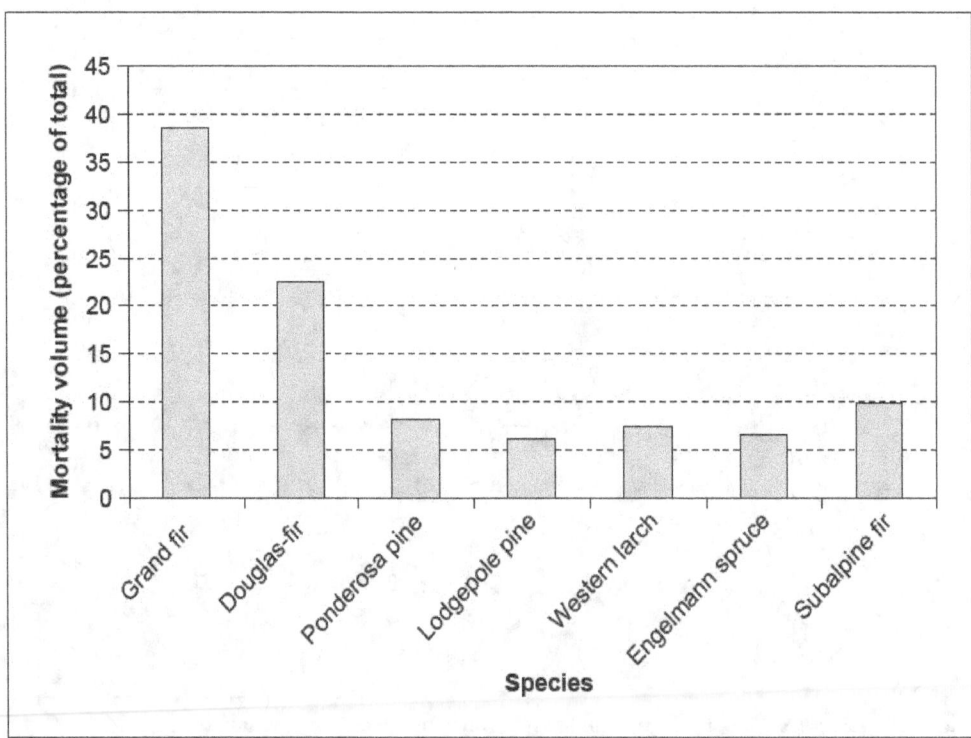

Figure 33—Percentage of total tree mortality volume, by species, Umatilla National Forest, 1996 to 2002 (occasion 1 and 2 data).

Most of the subalpine fir mortality was caused by the balsam woolly adelgid (*Adelges piceae* Ratzeburg), a small insect introduced from Europe more than 80 years ago. Much of the subalpine fir component in the interior Pacific Northwest has been damaged or killed by this insect since the mid 1980s (Livingston et al. 2000). Damage caused by balsam woolly adelgid can be difficult for forest inventory crews to identify, and mortality may often be attributed to unknown causes. In 2000, a statewide ground survey was conducted by the Oregon Department of Forestry to specifically determine the extent and severity of balsam woolly adelgid infestation in Oregon (Overhulser et al. 2004). A total of 71 plots with subalpine fir were visited on the Umatilla National Forest. Balsam woolly adelgid was found on 53 of the plots, and 24 of the plots had mortality attributed to balsam woolly adelgid.

The growth-to-mortality ratio can be viewed as a coarse-scale estimate of forest sustainability: if growth matches or exceeds mortality (and timber removals), then the forests could be viewed as sustainable (O'Laughlin and Cook 2003). The remeasurement data indicate that overall mortality and growth are statistically not significantly different. These estimates include a recent dramatic decline in federal timber harvest levels for the Umatilla National Forest (fig. 34) and reflect the forest health issues discussed previously (Johnson 1994, Mutch et al. 1993, Quigley 1992, Tanaka et al. 1995, Wickman 1992).

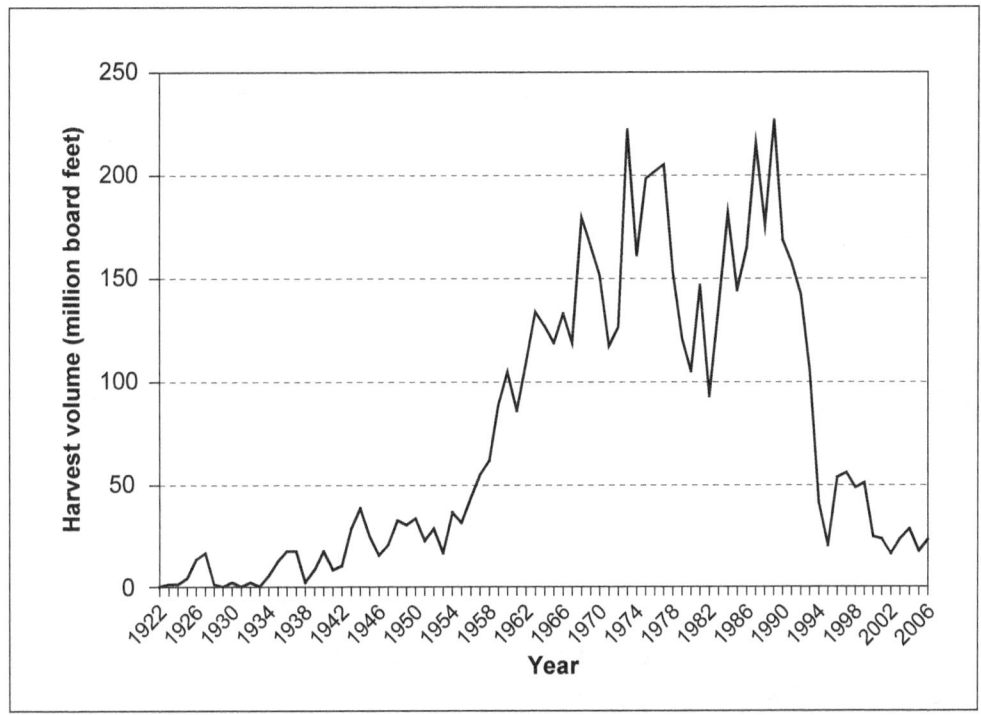

Figure 34—Umatilla National Forest timber harvest volume by year, 1922 to 2006. Source: Powell, D.C. 2007. Unpublished data. On file with: USDA Forest Service, Umatilla National Forest, 2517 SW Hailey Ave., Pendleton, OR 97801.

Site Class

The distribution of site classes across the forest could be considered another measure of productivity. Site class is a measure of an area's potential capability to produce woody biomass. It is determined by evaluating the mean annual increment (MAI) in cubic feet per acre (or other units of volume per area) per year, calculated by using published equations. Site classes on the forest range from site class 2, the most productive (MAI of 165 to 224 ft^3/acre per year), to site class 7, the lowest productivity level of forest land (MAI of <20 ft^3/acre per year). Figure 35 shows the distribution of site classes by forest type for the UNF. The greatest acreage (500,000 acres) is in site class 5, about 40 percent of all forest land. The other common site classes are classes 4 and 6, accounting for 19 percent and 29 percent of forest land, respectively. By forest type, grand fir and Douglas-fir tend to occupy the greatest proportion of acres on higher site classes (site classes 2 to 4).

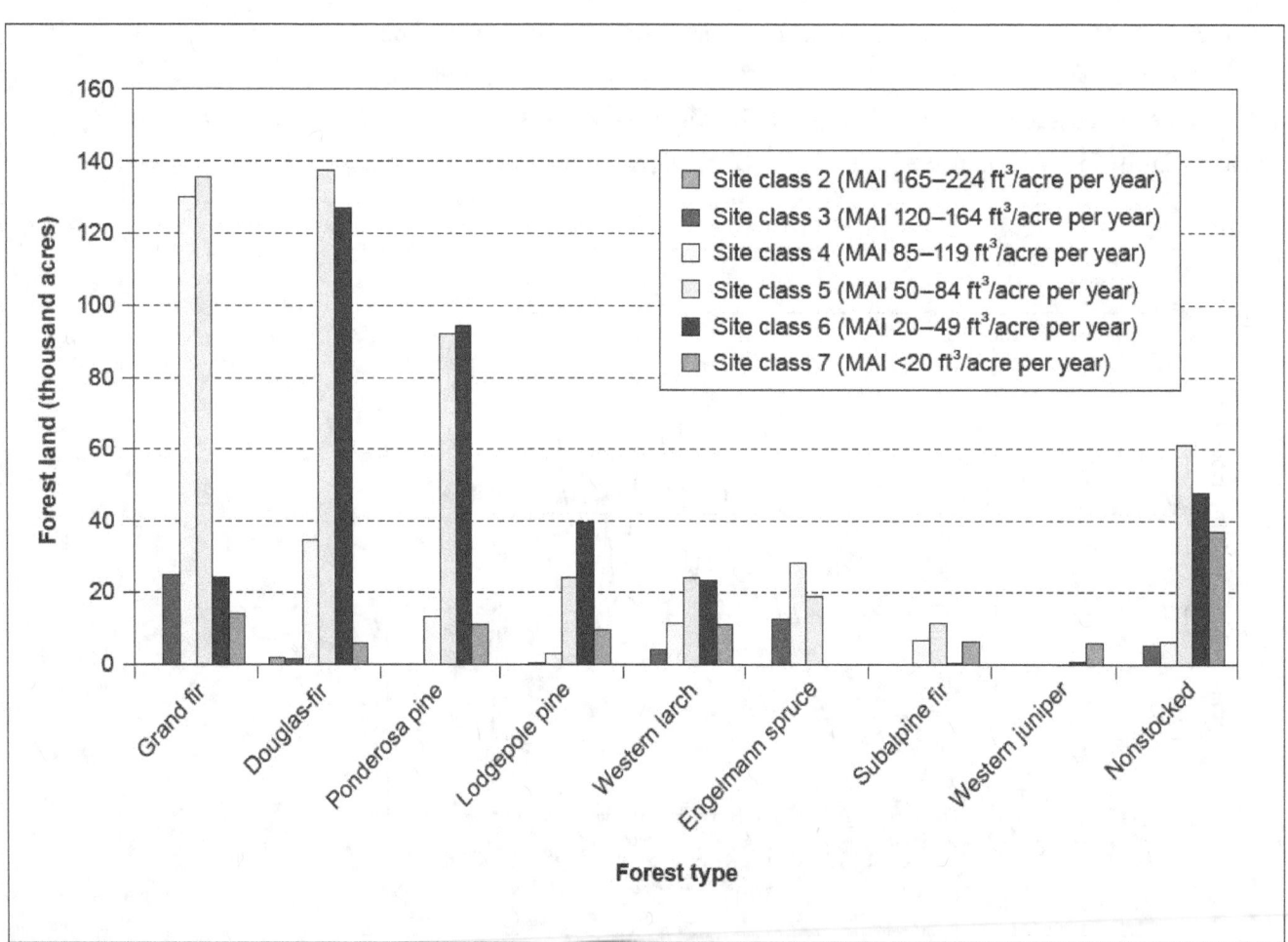

Figure 35—Forest land area by forest type and site class, Umatilla National Forest, 2002 (occasion 2 data only; MAI is mean annual increment).

This resource bulletin uses first- and second-occasion inventory data to describe forest conditions related to species composition, forest structure, stand density, woody biomass, and forest growth and mortality. Short-term trends for these condition indicators are interpreted in the context of forest health and productivity, including an assessment of how they were influenced by recent insect and disease outbreaks, and what they might represent in terms of future wildfire risk.

Common and Scientific Names

Common name	Scientific name
Black cottonwood	*Populus trichocarpa* Torr. & Gray
Douglas-fir	*Pseudotsuga menziesii* (Mirbel) Franco
Engelmann spruce	*Picea engelmannii* Parry ex Engelm.
Grand fir	*Abies grandis* (Dougl. ex D. Don) Lindl.
Lodgepole pine	*Pinus contorta* Dougl. ex Loud.
Pacific yew	*Taxus brevifolia* Nutt.
Ponderosa pine	*Pinus ponderosa* P. & C. Lawson
Subalpine fir	*Abies lasiocarpa* (Hook.) Nutt.
Western juniper	*Juniperus occidentalis* Hook.
Western larch	*Larix occidentalis* Nutt.
Western white pine	*Pinus monticola* Dougl. ex D. Don

Acknowledgments

The authors thank Alison Nelson, Glenn Fischer, Don Justice, Karen Waddell, and David Hatfield for their continued support and assistance in the preparation of this report.

The report was improved with critical reviews and suggestions made by Sally Campbell, Dave Azuma, Bill McArthur, Charlie Gobar, and Olaf Kugler.

Metric Equivalents

1 acre = 0.405 hectare (ha)
1 acre = 4046.86 square meters
1,000 acres = 404.7 hectares
1,000 cubic feet (ft^3) = 28.3 cubic meter
1 square foot per acre (ft^2/acre) = 0.229 square meter per hectare
1 cubic foot per acre (ft^3/acre) = 0.07 cubic meters per hectare (m^3/ha)
1 foot (ft) = 0.3048 meters (m)
1 inch = 2.54 centimeters (cm)
1 mile (mi) = 1.609 kilometers (km)
1 pound per cubic foot (lb/ft^3) = 16.02 kilograms per cubic meter (kg/m^3)
1 ton = 907 kilograms
1 ton per acre = 2.24 tonnes per hectare

References

Anderson, E.W.; Borman, M.M.; Krueger, W.C. 1998. The ecological provinces of Oregon: a treatise on the basic ecological geography of the state. SR 990. Corvallis, OR: Oregon Agricultural Experiment Station. 138 p.

Bull, E.L.; Parks, C.G.; Torgersen, T.R. 1997. Trees and logs important to wildlife in the interior Columbia River basin. Gen. Tech. Rep. PNW-GTR-391. Portland, OR: U.S. Department of Agriculture, Forest Service, Pacific Northwest Research Station. 55 p.

Clarke, S.E.; Bryce, S.A., eds. 1997. Hierarchical subdivisions of the Columbia Plateau and Blue Mountains ecoregions, Oregon and Washington. Gen. Tech. Rep. PNW-GTR-395. Portland, OR: U.S. Department of Agriculture, Forest Service, Pacific Northwest Research Station. 114 p.

Eyre, F.H. 1980. Forest cover types of the United States and Canada. Washington, DC: Society of American Foresters. 148 p.

Fiedler, C.E.; Keegan, C.E., III; Woodall, C.W.; Morgan, T.A. 2004. A strategic assessment of crown fire hazard in Montana: potential effectiveness and costs of hazard reduction treatments. Gen. Tech. Rep. PNW-GTR-622. Portland, OR: U.S. Department of Agriculture, Forest Service, Pacific Northwest Research Station. 48 p.

Fried, J.S.; Christensen, G.; Weyermann, D.; Barbour, R.J.; Fight, R.; Hiserote, B.; Pinjuv, G. 2005. Modeling opportunities and feasibility of siting wood-fired electrical generating facilities to facilitate landscape-scale fuel treatment with FIA BioSum. In: Bevers, M.; Barrett, T.M., comps. Systems analysis in forest resources: proceedings of the 2003 symposium. Gen. Tech. Rep. PNW-GTR-656. Portland, OR: U.S. Department of Agriculture, Forest Service, Pacific Northwest Research Station: 195–204.

Gedney, D.R.; Azuma, D.L.; Bolsinger, C.L.; McKay, N. 1999. Western juniper in eastern Oregon. Gen. Tech. Rep. PNW-GTR-464. Portland, OR: U.S. Department of Agriculture, Forest Service, Pacific Northwest Research Station. 53 p.

Johnson, C.G., Jr. 1994. Forest health in the Blue Mountains: a plant ecologist's perspective on ecosystem processes and biological diversity. Gen. Tech. Rep. PNW-GTR-339. Portland, OR: U.S. Department of Agriculture, Forest Service, Pacific Northwest Research Station. 24 p.

Johnson, M.D. 1998. Region 6 inventory and monitoring system: field procedures for the Current Vegetation Survey. Version 2.03. Portland, OR: U.S. Department of Agriculture, Forest Service, Pacific Northwest Region. 143 p.

Johnson, M.D. 2001. Region 6 inventory and monitoring system: field procedures for the Current Vegetation Survey. Version 2.04. Portland, OR: U.S. Department of Agriculture, Forest Service, Pacific Northwest Region. 151 p.

Livingston, R.L.; Dewey, J.E.; Beckman, D.P.; Stipe, L.E. 2000. Distribution of the balsam woolly adelgid in Idaho. Western Journal of Applied Forestry. 15(4): 227–231.

Max, T.A.; Schreuder, H.T.; Hazard, J.W.; Oswald, D.D.; Teply, J.; Alegria, J. 1996. The Pacific Northwest Region vegetation and inventory monitoring system. Res. Pap. PNW-RP-493. Portland, OR: U.S. Department of Agriculture, Forest Service, Pacific Northwest Research Station. 22 p.

Mutch, R.W.; Arno, S.F.; Brown, J.K.; Carlson, C.E.; Ottmar, R.D.; Peterson, J.L. 1993. Forest health in the Blue Mountains: a management strategy for fire-adapted ecosystems. Gen. Tech. Rep. PNW-GTR-310. Portland, OR: U.S. Department of Agriculture, Forest Service, Pacific Northwest Research Station. 14 p.

O'Laughlin, J.O.; Cook, P.S. 2003. Inventory-based forest health indicators: implications for national forest management. Journal of Forestry. 101(2): 11–17.

Overhulser, D.L.; Ragenovich, I.R.; McWilliams, M.; Willhite, E.A. 2004. Balsam woolly adelgid occurrence on true fir in Oregon. Pest Management Report. [Salem, OR]: Oregon Department of Forestry. 7 p.

Powell, D.C. 1994. Effects of the 1980s western spruce budworm outbreak on the Malheur National Forest in northeastern Oregon. R6-FI&D-TP-12-94. Portland, OR: U.S. Department of Agriculture, Forest Service, Pacific Northwest Region, Forest Insects and Diseases Group. 176 p.

Powell, D.C. 2005. Tree density thresholds related to crown fire susceptibility. 20 p. Unpublished report. On file with: USDA Forest Service, Umatilla National Forest, 2517 SW Hailey Avenue, Pendleton, OR 97801.

Quigley, T.M. 1992. Forest health in the Blue Mountains: social and economic perspectives. Gen. Tech. Rep. PNW-GTR-296. Portland, OR: U.S. Department of Agriculture, Forest Service, Pacific Northwest Research Station. 9 p.

Reinhardt, E.D.; Crookston, N.L., tech. eds. 2003. The Fire and Fuels Extension to the Forest Vegetation Simulator. Gen. Tech. Rep. RMRS-GTR-116. Ogden, UT: U.S. Department of Agriculture, Forest Service, Rocky Mountain Research Station. 209 p.

Sampson, R.N.; Adams, D.L.; Enzer, M.J. 1994. Assessing forest ecosystem health in the inland West. New York: Food Products Press. 461 p.

Scott, J.H.; Reinhardt, E.D. 2001. Assessing crown fire potential by linking models of surface and crown fire behavior. Res. Pap. RMRS-RP-29. Fort Collins, CO: U.S. Department of Agriculture, Forest Service, Rocky Mountain Research Station. 59 p.

Tanaka, J.A.; Starr, G.L.; Quigley, T.M. 1995. Strategies and recommendations for addressing forest health issues in the Blue Mountains of Oregon and Washington. Gen. Tech. Rep. PNW-GTR-350. Portland, OR: U.S. Department of Agriculture, Forest Service, Pacific Northwest Research Station. 18 p.

Teply, J. 1981. Umatilla National Forest; summary tables for timber resource inventory. Pendleton, OR: U.S. Department of Agriculture, Forest Service. [Three, 3-ring binders; unconventional pagination].

Thomas, J.W.; Anderson, R.G.; Maser, C.; Bull, E.L. 1979. Snags. In: Thomas, J.W., tech. ed. Wildlife habitats in managed forests: the Blue Mountains of Oregon and Washington. Agric. Handb. 553. Washington, DC: U.S. Department of Agriculture, Forest Service: 60–77.

U.S. Department of Agriculture, Forest Service. 2005. Forest Vegetation Simulator (FVS) Web site. Fort Collins, CO, Forest Management Service Center. http://www.fs.fed.us/fmsc/fvs/ (January 2007).

Waddell K.L.; Hiserote, B., comps. 2005. The PNW-FIA integrated database user guide and documentation: a database of forest inventory information for California, Oregon, and Washington; version 2.0. Unpublished report. On file with: USDA Forest Service, Forest Inventory and Analysis Program, Pacific Northwest Research Station, 620 SW Main, Suite 400, P.O. Box 3890, Portland, OR 97205.

Wickman, B.E. 1992. Forest health in the Blue Mountains: the influence of insects and disease. Gen. Tech. Rep. PNW-GTR-295. Portland, OR: U.S. Department of Agriculture, Forest Service, Pacific Northwest Research Station. 15 p.